TABLE OF CONTENTS

1.	INTRODUCTION	
2.	Understanding the basics of first principle thinking: why it's important.	
3.	The history of first principle thinking: How this mode of reasoning has been used throughout history and across cultures.	11
4.	Key principles of first principle thinking: Breaking down the essential elements of this way of thinking.	18
5.	Examples of first principle thinking in action: Case studies and real-world examples of how first principle thinking has been applied.	25
6.	Common misconceptions about first principle thinking: Addressing myths and misunderstandings about this mode of reasoning.	33
7.	Applying first principle thinking to personal growth and decision-making: How to use this approach to make better choices in your own life.	39
8.	Overcoming cognitive biases with first principle thinking: How to use this mode of reasoning to overcome the limitations of our own minds.	47
9.	The role of first principle thinking in innovation and creativity: How first principle thinking can be used to generate novel ideas.	54
10.	Using first principle thinking to solve complex problems: How this mode of reasoning can be applied to tackle big, difficult problems.	61
11.	Combining first principle thinking with other problem-solving approaches: How to integrate first principle thinking with other problem-solving methods.	67
12.	The future of first principle thinking: Exploring how this mode of reasoning might evolve and be applied in the years to come.	74
13.	Critiques of first principle thinking: Examining the potential downsides and limitations of this way of thinking.	82
14.	Cultivating a first principle mindset: Tips and exercises for developing a first principle mindset and making it a habit.	89
15.	Debating and challenging assumptions through first principle thinking: How to use first principle thinking to question the status quo.	96
16.	Applying first principle thinking to fields beyond science and engineering: How first principle thinking can be applied to areas like philosophy, business, and politics.	103
17.	CONCLUSION	110

INTRODUCTION:

In our rapidly changing world, it has become increasingly important to think critically and creatively to solve complex problems and make sound decisions. While many traditional problem-solving methods rely on past experiences or existing knowledge, first principle thinking is a powerful tool that encourages us to question assumptions and approach problems from a fresh perspective.

In this book, "Think Outside the Books: A Guide to First Principle Thinking," we will explore the concept of first principle thinking in depth, providing practical tips and strategies for applying this approach to a variety of fields, from science and technology to business and philosophy. We will examine the key principles underlying first principle thinking, including the importance of questioning assumptions, breaking down problems into their fundamental components, and generating new insights and ideas based on those components.

Throughout the book, we will provide numerous examples and case studies to illustrate the power of first principle thinking in action. We will also offer guidance on how to cultivate and develop the skills needed to become an effective first principle thinker, including critical thinking, analytical reasoning, and creativity.

Whether you are a scientist looking to push the boundaries of knowledge, an entrepreneur seeking new opportunities for growth and innovation, or simply a curious individual interested in exploring the world from a fresh perspective, this book is for you. So let's dive in and start thinking outside the books!

CHAPTER 1

Understanding the basics of first principle thinking: What it is, how it works, and why it's important.

1. Definition of first principle thinking and how it differs from other problem-solving approaches.

First principle thinking is a mode of reasoning that involves breaking down a problem or situation into its most fundamental elements and building up from there using logic and reason. It differs from other problem-solving approaches, such as analogy-based thinking or trial-and-error, in that it seeks to uncover the underlying principles or laws governing the situation rather than relying on preconceived ideas or assumptions.

According to a survey conducted by McKinsey, 82% of executives believe that a company's ability to innovate is essential for growth and success. First principle thinking can be a powerful tool for innovation, as it encourages us to question assumptions and think outside the box.

One example of first principle thinking in action is the development of SpaceX's reusable rockets. Rather than accepting the conventional wisdom that rockets are single-use and must be discarded after a single launch, Elon Musk and his team applied first principle thinking to the problem. They broke down the cost of a rocket into its component parts and identified the most expensive components, such as the engines and fuel tanks. They then worked to develop new technologies that would enable these components to be reused, ultimately leading to significant cost savings.

Another example of first principle thinking in action is the development of the iPhone by Apple. Instead of simply trying to improve upon existing cell phones, Apple's designers applied first principle thinking to the problem. They identified the fundamental elements of a phone, such as the screen and the buttons, and reimagined them from scratch. The result was a revolutionary product that changed the mobile phone industry forever.

To apply first principle thinking in your own life or work, start by identifying the assumptions and preconceptions that may be limiting your thinking. Ask yourself "why" questions to get to the root cause of a problem or situation, and use logic and reason to evaluate different solutions or approaches. Consider alternative perspectives and viewpoints, and remain open to revising your assumptions based on new evidence or insights. By adopting a first principle mindset, you can unlock new possibilities and achieve breakthrough results.

2. Explanation of the origins and history of first principle thinking and how it has been used in various fields.

The concept of first principle thinking has its roots in philosophy, dating back to the ancient Greek philosopher Aristotle. Aristotle argued that all knowledge can be traced back to fundamental principles, which he called "first principles." This idea was later developed by other philosophers, including René Descartes and Immanuel Kant.

In the modern era, first principle thinking has been applied in various fields, including science, engineering, and business. In the field of science, first principle thinking involves using fundamental laws and principles to understand complex phenomena. For example, in physics, first principle thinking is used to derive equations that describe the behavior of particles and forces.

In engineering, first principle thinking is used to design new products and technologies. For example, in the automotive industry, engineers use first principle thinking to understand the physics of a vehicle and design more fuel-efficient engines and lightweight materials.

In business, first principle thinking is used to identify new opportunities and create innovative solutions. For example, when Elon Musk founded SpaceX, he used first principle thinking to identify the fundamental problems with the existing space industry and develop a new approach to space travel.

According to a survey conducted by McKinsey, 70% of executives believe that innovation is a top-three priority for their organization. First principle thinking can be a powerful tool for innovation, as it encourages us to question assumptions and think outside the box.

One example of first principle thinking in action is the development of Tesla's electric cars. Rather than trying to improve upon existing gas-powered cars, Tesla's engineers used first principle thinking to design a completely new type of vehicle. They started by asking fundamental questions about the physics of a car, such as "How can we make it more energy efficient?" and "How can we reduce the weight of the vehicle?" By using first principle thinking, they were able to create a breakthrough product that disrupted the automotive industry.

Another example of first principle thinking in action is the development of Airbnb. Instead of trying to compete with traditional hotels, the founders of Airbnb used first principle thinking to identify the fundamental problems with the existing hospitality industry, such as high prices and limited availability. They then created a new platform that connected travelers with local hosts, offering a more affordable and authentic travel experience.

In summary, first principle thinking has a rich history dating back to ancient philosophy, and has been applied in various fields throughout history. By breaking down complex problems into their most fundamental elements, and using logic and reason to build up from there, first principle thinking can be a powerful tool for innovation and problem-solving.

3. Overview of the key characteristics of first principle thinking, such as starting from fundamental truths and questioning assumptions.

First principle thinking is a mode of reasoning that involves breaking down complex problems into their fundamental elements and re-evaluating assumptions to arrive at new, innovative solutions. Some of the key characteristics of first principle thinking include:
Starting from fundamental truths: Rather than relying on existing assumptions or conventional wisdom, first principle thinking begins with the most basic, fundamental truths about a problem or situation.

Questioning assumptions: First principle thinking involves challenging assumptions and beliefs that may be limiting our ability to solve problems or innovate.

Using logic and reasoning: First principle thinking relies on logical and analytical reasoning to arrive at new insights and solutions.

Being open-minded: First principle thinking requires a willingness to question and challenge our own beliefs and assumptions, as well as those of others.

Focusing on the essential: First principle thinking involves breaking down problems into their essential components and evaluating each one individually.

Examples of first principle thinking in action can be found across a range of fields. For instance, Elon Musk, the CEO of SpaceX and Tesla, has used first principle thinking to drive innovation in the aerospace and automotive industries. Rather than accepting the high costs of traditional rocket manufacturing, Musk broke down the problem into its most basic elements and developed a new approach that dramatically lowered costs. Similarly, he used first principle thinking to design the Tesla Model S electric car from scratch, rather than simply improving on existing gasoline-powered vehicles.

Another example of first principle thinking can be found in the field of medicine. In the early 20th century, doctors believed that stomach ulcers were caused by stress and spicy foods. However, Australian physician Barry Marshall challenged this assumption and used first principle thinking to prove that ulcers were actually caused by bacteria. This insight led to new treatments that have saved countless lives.

In summary, first principle thinking is a powerful problem-solving approach that has been used in a variety of fields to drive innovation and progress. By starting from fundamental truths and questioning assumptions, we can unlock new insights and solutions that would be impossible to achieve through conventional thinking.

4. Discussion of the importance of first principle thinking in enabling breakthrough innovations and discoveries.

First principle thinking has played a crucial role in some of the most ground-breaking innovations and discoveries in history. For example, the invention of the steam engine, which revolutionized transportation and industry, was made possible by first principle thinking. James Watt, the inventor of the steam engine, didn't just try to improve on existing steam engines. Instead, he broke down the problem to its fundamental principles and designed an entirely new engine that was much more efficient.

Another example of the power of first principle thinking is the discovery of DNA's structure. In 1953, James Watson and Francis Crick used first principles to deduce the double helix structure of DNA. Instead of just trying to fit the available data into existing models, they asked themselves: what are the basic building blocks of DNA, and how can they be arranged to form a stable structure?

In more recent times, companies like SpaceX and Tesla have also used first principle thinking to drive innovation. SpaceX's reusable rockets, for example, were made possible by breaking down the problem of space travel into its most fundamental components and designing a rocket that could be reused, rather than building expensive, disposable rockets every time.

Overall, first principle thinking has been shown to be a powerful tool for enabling breakthrough innovations and discoveries because it enables people to look beyond existing solutions and question their underlying assumptions. By starting from fundamental truths, people can arrive at entirely new and innovative solutions to problems.

5. Examples of how first principle thinking has been used in science, engineering, and technology, such as the development of the steam engine or the discovery of DNA.

First principle thinking has been used extensively in science, engineering, and technology, leading to many ground-breaking discoveries and innovations. Here are some notable examples:

Steam Engine: In the 18th century, the steam engine was invented by James Watt using first principle thinking. Instead of improving the existing steam engines, he broke down the problem to its fundamental principles and designed an entirely new engine that was much more efficient.

DNA Structure: In 1953, James Watson and Francis Crick used first principles to deduce the double helix structure of DNA. By starting from fundamental principles and questioning assumptions, they were able to arrive at a revolutionary discovery that has had a profound impact on biology and medicine.

SpaceX: SpaceX, the rocket company founded by Elon Musk, has used first principle thinking to make space travel more accessible and affordable. For example, instead of using traditional manufacturing methods, SpaceX designed and built its rockets in-house using reusable parts, resulting in a significant reduction in costs.

Tesla: Tesla, the electric car company founded by Elon Musk, has used first principle thinking to improve the efficiency and performance of electric vehicles. By starting from fundamental principles, Tesla has been able to design and manufacture electric cars that have a longer range, faster acceleration, and lower cost than their competitors.

Solar Energy: The development of solar energy is another example of first principle thinking in action. By breaking down the problem to its fundamental principles and designing more efficient solar panels, scientists and engineers have been able to significantly reduce the cost and increase the efficiency of solar energy.

Overall, first principle thinking has been instrumental in driving innovation and progress in science, engineering, and technology. By questioning assumptions and starting from fundamental principles, people have been able to arrive at revolutionary discoveries and solutions to complex problems.

6. The role of first principle thinking in entrepreneurship and business innovation, such as identifying new markets and creating disruptive business models.

First principle thinking can also be applied in entrepreneurship and business innovation to identify new opportunities and create disruptive business models. This approach requires entrepreneurs to question the assumptions that underlie existing business models and industry norms.

One example of first principle thinking in business innovation is the case of Airbnb. The founders of Airbnb, Brian Chesky and Joe Gebbia, used first principle thinking to challenge the assumption that people only need traditional hotel rooms when traveling. They broke down the fundamental needs of travelers, such as a safe and comfortable place to stay, and found a new way to provide that through peer-to-peer home-sharing.

Another example is the electric car company, Tesla. Elon Musk applied first principle thinking to the design and production of electric cars, questioning the assumptions about what a car should look like and how it should be powered. This led to the creation of electric cars that had longer ranges, faster acceleration, and a sleek design.

According to a survey by McKinsey, companies that consistently apply first principle thinking in their innovation process are more likely to achieve breakthrough innovation and superior financial performance. Additionally, companies that use first principle thinking in their innovation process are more likely to create disruptive business models and outperform their competitors.

Overall, first principle thinking can be a powerful tool for entrepreneurs and businesses to identify new opportunities, challenge assumptions, and create disruptive business models that drive innovation and financial success.

7. The limitations of relying on analogies or existing knowledge versus first principle thinking in solving complex problems.

When facing complex problems, people often rely on analogies or existing knowledge to find solutions. However, this approach has its limitations, as it can lead to assumptions and biases that prevent creative solutions from emerging. This is where first principle thinking can be particularly useful, as it encourages us to start from fundamental truths and question our assumptions.

For example, consider the problem of designing a better battery for electric cars. An analogy-based approach might involve looking at existing battery technologies and trying to improve upon them. However, this approach may be limited by the assumptions and biases inherent in current battery designs. On the other hand, a first principle approach might involve breaking down the problem into its fundamental components, such as the chemistry and physics of energy storage, and exploring new materials and technologies that could enable more efficient and cost-effective batteries.

This approach has been successfully used in many fields. One example is Elon Musk's SpaceX, which used first principle thinking to design rockets that could be reused, significantly reducing the cost of space launches. Another example is the development of the modern airplane by the Wright brothers, who used first principle thinking to break down the problem of flight into its fundamental principles and design a machine that could achieve it.

While analogies and existing knowledge can be helpful in problem-solving, they should not be relied on exclusively. First principle thinking can be a powerful tool for breaking down complex problems and generating innovative solutions that would not be possible otherwise.

8. Explanation of how first principle thinking can be used to generate creative and unconventional ideas by breaking down a problem into its basic elements.

First principle thinking can be a powerful tool for generating creative and unconventional ideas. By breaking down a problem into its most fundamental elements, first principle thinking allows for a more nuanced understanding of the problem at hand, and can lead to insights and ideas that may not have been apparent before.

For example, consider the case of SpaceX and their development of reusable rockets. Traditional thinking in the aerospace industry had always been to discard rockets after a single use, as the cost of refurbishing and reusing them was thought to be too high. However, SpaceX founder Elon Musk applied first principle thinking to the problem and determined that the true cost of launching rockets was not in the materials themselves, but in the complex manufacturing processes and supply chains required to produce them. By developing a reusable rocket that could drastically reduce the costs of manufacturing and supply chain, SpaceX was able to disrupt the aerospace industry and achieve its goal of making space travel more affordable and accessible.

Another example is the story of James Dyson, who revolutionized the vacuum cleaner industry by applying first principle thinking. Dyson was dissatisfied with the performance of his own vacuum cleaner, which relied on a traditional filter that quickly became clogged with dirt and reduced suction. Rather than accepting this limitation, Dyson applied first principle thinking and determined that the true problem was not the filter, but the fact that it allowed dirt particles to escape back into the air. By developing a vacuum cleaner that used cyclonic separation to filter dirt and maintain suction, Dyson was able to create a product that was more efficient, effective, and desirable to consumers.

These examples demonstrate how first principle thinking can lead to creative and unconventional solutions by challenging traditional assumptions and focusing on the fundamental elements of a problem.

9. Discussion of the cognitive biases that can prevent us from using first principle thinking effectively, and how to overcome them.

Cognitive biases are mental shortcuts that our brains use to simplify decision-making, but they can also lead us to make errors in judgment. These biases can be especially problematic when attempting to use first principle thinking, which requires breaking down problems into their most basic elements and questioning assumptions. Here are some common cognitive biases that can impede effective use of first principle thinking:

Confirmation bias: This occurs when we seek out information that confirms our preexisting beliefs and ignore evidence that contradicts them. When using first principle thinking, it is important to be open to considering all possible solutions, even if they challenge our assumptions.

Availability bias: This is the tendency to overvalue information that is readily available to us and undervalue information that is more difficult to obtain. When using first principle thinking, it is important to gather all relevant information, even if it requires more effort.

Anchoring bias: This occurs when we rely too heavily on the first piece of information we receive, even if it is not the most accurate or relevant. When using first principle thinking, it is important to remain open-minded and not become fixated on a single idea or solution.

To overcome these biases, it is important to consciously recognize them and actively work to counteract them. This can involve seeking out diverse perspectives and information sources, challenging assumptions, and considering all possible solutions, even those that may be unconventional or uncomfortable to consider.

10. An overview of how to apply first principle thinking in practical situations, such as decision-making, problem-solving, and strategy development.

First principle thinking is a powerful approach to problem-solving that can be applied in a variety of practical situations. Here are some ways to apply first principle thinking in practice:

Decision-making: When faced with a difficult decision, start by breaking down the problem into its fundamental components. Then, use first principle thinking to analyze each component independently and make a decision based on the most basic and fundamental facts.

Problem-solving: When trying to solve a complex problem, begin by breaking it down into its most basic elements. Then, use first principle thinking to examine each element individually and come up with creative solutions based on the most fundamental truths.

Strategy development: When developing a new strategy, start by examining the underlying assumptions and principles that are driving the current approach. Then, use first principle thinking to challenge these assumptions and develop a new strategy based on the most basic and fundamental facts.

For example, Elon Musk used first principle thinking when he founded SpaceX. Rather than accepting the high cost of rockets as a given, he broke down the cost of each component and used first principle thinking to find new and innovative ways to reduce costs. This led to the development of the Falcon 1 rocket, which was significantly cheaper than existing rockets and allowed SpaceX to become a major player in the space industry.

Another example is Airbnb, which used first principle thinking to disrupt the hospitality industry. Rather than accepting the traditional hotel model as the only way to provide accommodation, the founders broke down the problem into its most basic components and found a way to connect travelers with people who had spare rooms. This led to the development of a new business model that has since revolutionized the travel industry.

In practical situations, first principle thinking can be used to challenge assumptions, generate new ideas, and develop innovative solutions to complex problems. By breaking down problems into their most basic elements and analyzing each component independently, it is possible to arrive at truly novel and creative solutions that would not be possible using other problem-solving approaches.

CHAPTER 2

The History Of First Principle Thinking: How This Mode Of Reasoning Has Been Used Throughout History And Across Cultures.

1. An overview of the origins of first principle thinking in ancient Greek philosophy and its role in the work of philosophers like Aristotle and Plato.

First principle thinking can trace its roots back to ancient Greek philosophy, particularly the work of Aristotle and Plato. Aristotle believed that all knowledge could be derived from first principles, which were basic, self-evident truths that did not require further explanation or justification. Plato, on the other hand, believed that knowledge of the forms or idealized versions of things was necessary to truly understand the world.

These ideas have had a profound impact on Western philosophy and have been influential in fields like science and mathematics. For example, the scientific method, which involves starting with a hypothesis and testing it through experimentation, is often seen as a form of first principle thinking. Similarly, mathematical proofs rely on axioms, which are basic principles that are taken as self-evident truths.

In recent years, first principle thinking has gained renewed attention in the business world, particularly in the tech industry. Entrepreneurs like Elon Musk have used first principle thinking to develop innovative products and disrupt existing industries. For example, Musk used first principle thinking to design the Tesla Model S by starting with the fundamental principles of physics and engineering, rather than relying on existing automotive design conventions.

Overall, the origins of first principle thinking in ancient Greek philosophy demonstrate the enduring influence of this mode of reasoning and its applicability to a wide range of fields.

2. Explanation of how first principle thinking has been used in other philosophical traditions, such as Taoism and Zen Buddhism.

While first principle thinking is commonly associated with Western philosophy, it has also been used in other philosophical traditions, including Taoism and Zen Buddhism.

In Taoism, first principle thinking is closely related to the concept of the Tao, or the ultimate reality that underlies all things. The Tao is often described as ineffable and indescribable, but it can be understood through the process of direct experience and intuitive understanding. This approach is similar to first principle thinking in that it seeks to identify the essential nature of things by stripping away extraneous assumptions and concepts.

In Zen Buddhism, first principle thinking is known as shoshin, which means "beginner's mind." This refers to the idea of approaching each situation with an open and curious mindset, without preconceived notions or assumptions. By doing so, one is better able to see things as they truly are, rather than through the filter of one's beliefs or expectations. This is similar to the first principle thinking approach of questioning assumptions and starting with a blank slate.

Overall, these philosophical traditions demonstrate that first principle thinking is not limited to a particular culture or time period, but rather is a fundamental approach to understanding the world around us.

3. Examples of how first principle thinking has been applied in scientific and mathematical breakthroughs, such as the work of Galileo, Newton, and Einstein.

First principle thinking has played a crucial role in scientific and mathematical breakthroughs throughout history. For instance, Galileo Galilei used first principle thinking to establish the basic principles of motion, including the law of inertia, which formed the foundation for Isaac Newton's development of classical mechanics. Newton, in turn, used first principles to derive his laws of motion and law of universal gravitation, which explained the motion of celestial bodies.

Albert Einstein's theory of relativity also relied on first principle thinking. Einstein questioned the fundamental assumptions of Newtonian mechanics and developed a new theory based on the concept of the constancy of the speed of light and the equivalence of inertial frames of reference.

In mathematics, first principle thinking has led to some of the most significant advances in the field. For instance, René Descartes used first principles to develop the Cartesian coordinate system, which paved the way for the development of analytical geometry. Mathematicians such as Euclid, Pythagoras, and Archimedes also used first principles to establish the basic axioms of geometry and to derive important mathematical theorems.

Overall, first principle thinking has played a critical role in advancing scientific and mathematical knowledge, allowing researchers to question fundamental assumptions and develop new models and theories based on basic principles.

4. Discussion of the role of first principle thinking in the development of modern engineering and technology, such as the steam engine and the computer.

First principle thinking has played a crucial role in the development of modern engineering and technology. The steam engine, which powered the Industrial Revolution, is an excellent example of this. In the late 17th century, the French physicist Denis Papin began experimenting with steam to create a more efficient method of powering machines. He developed a device called a "piston and cylinder" engine, which used steam to push a piston back and forth inside a cylinder. However, the engine was inefficient and unreliable, and it was not until the Scottish engineer James Watt applied first principle thinking to the problem that the steam engine became a practical and reliable source of power.

Watt began by breaking down the problem into its basic elements and questioning the assumptions underlying Papin's design. He realized that the key to improving the efficiency of the steam engine was to keep the cylinder as hot as possible throughout the entire cycle of the engine. To achieve this, he introduced a separate condenser, which allowed the cylinder to remain hot while the steam was condensed in a separate chamber. Watt's new design was vastly more efficient and reliable than Papin's, and it became the basis for the steam engines that powered the Industrial Revolution.

Similarly, the development of the computer was made possible by first principle thinking. In the mid-20th century, a group of engineers and mathematicians led by John von Neumann began to design the first electronic computers. They realized that the key to creating a programmable computer was to break down the problem into its basic elements and design a machine that could perform simple operations on binary numbers.

The result was the von Neumann architecture, which is still used in computers today. This architecture consists of a central processing unit (CPU), memory, and input/output devices. The CPU performs simple operations on binary numbers stored in memory, and the input/output devices allow the to interact with the machine. By applying first principle thinking to the problem of computer design, von Neumann and his colleagues were able to create a machine that could perform complex calculations and processes, revolutionizing fields like science, engineering, and business.

Overall, first principle thinking has been essential to the development of modern engineering and technology, allowing innovators to break down complex problems into their basic elements and design practical and efficient solutions.

5. *An overview of how first principle thinking has been applied in economics and business, such as the work of economist Joseph Schumpeter and entrepreneur Elon Musk.*

First principle thinking has also been applied in the fields of economics and business to drive innovation and success. Economist Joseph Schumpeter, for instance, used first principle thinking to develop his theory of "creative destruction," which suggests that economic growth and innovation come from the destruction of old industries and the creation of new ones.

Entrepreneur Elon Musk is another prominent figure who has applied first principle thinking to his businesses. When developing SpaceX, Musk used first principles to question the conventional approach to rocket engineering and create a new, more efficient design. This approach allowed SpaceX to drastically reduce the cost of rocket launches and revolutionize the space industry.

In his work with Tesla, Musk has also used first principle thinking to address the challenges of electric vehicle (EV) development. Rather than simply trying to improve on existing EV technology, Musk and his team questioned the fundamental assumptions of how batteries and charging infrastructure should work, resulting in innovations like the Supercharger network and longer-lasting batteries.

These examples demonstrate how first principle thinking can be applied in economics and business to challenge assumptions, drive innovation, and create value.

6. Explanation of how first principle thinking has been used in political and social movements, such as the American Revolution and the Civil Rights Movement.

First principle thinking has played an important role in various political and social movements throughout history. In the American Revolution, the Founding Fathers used first principle thinking to challenge the fundamental assumption that the British monarchy had the right to rule over the American colonies without their consent. They argued that all people had the right to self-governance and that this was a fundamental truth that could not be compromised. This first principle thinking ultimately led to the establishment of the United States as an independent nation.

Similarly, in the Civil Rights Movement, leaders such as Martin Luther King Jr. used first principle thinking to challenge the assumption that African Americans were inferior to white Americans and should be treated as second-class citizens. They argued that all people were created equal and that this fundamental truth should guide our laws and policies. This first principle thinking ultimately led to the end of segregation and the passage of civil rights legislation.

Overall, first principle thinking has been a powerful tool for political and social change throughout history. By starting with fundamental truths and questioning assumptions, it has enabled people to challenge the status quo and bring about meaningful transformation.

7. Examples of how first principle thinking has been used in art and creativity, such as the work of Picasso and other modernist artists.

First principle thinking, while often associated with scientific and technical fields, can also be applied to art and creativity. Artists and designers have used first principle thinking to break down traditional ideas and approaches, leading to new and innovative works.

One example of first principle thinking in art is the work of Pablo Picasso, who is considered one of the founders of the Cubist movement. Cubism involved breaking down traditional representational art into its basic elements and reconstructing it in a new way. This approach was based on the idea of "analytic cubism," which sought to break down the visual world into its basic shapes and forms.

Another example is the work of modernist artists like Marcel Duchamp, who used first principle thinking to challenge traditional ideas of art and beauty. Duchamp's "readymades" were ordinary objects that he recontextualized as art by removing them from their original context and presenting them in a gallery setting.

In the field of design, first principle thinking has been used to create innovative and functional products. For example, the design of the first Apple Macintosh computer was based on first principle thinking, with its creators starting from scratch to create a new and revolutionary product.

In these examples, first principle thinking allowed artists and designers to break down traditional approaches and create something entirely new and innovative. By questioning assumptions and starting from fundamental truths, they were able to push the boundaries of their respective fields and create works that challenged and changed the way people think about art and design.

8. Discussion of how first principle thinking has been used in moral and ethical reasoning, such as the work of Kant and other philosophers.

First principle thinking, or reasoning from first principles, has also been used in the realm of moral and ethical reasoning. Immanuel Kant, one of the most influential philosophers in the Western tradition, used a form of first principle thinking in his ethical theory, which he called the "Categorical Imperative." The Categorical Imperative is based on the idea that we should act in a way that we would want others to act towards us, and that we should treat other people as ends in themselves, rather than as means to our own ends.

Kant believed that these principles were self-evident and did not require any further justification. He argued that they were necessary for any rational agent to act morally, and that they could be derived through reason alone. In this sense, Kant's ethical theory can be seen as an example of first principle thinking in the realm of morality.

Other philosophers have also used first principle thinking in their moral and ethical reasoning. For example, John Rawls, in his book "A Theory of Justice," used a form of first principle thinking to derive his theory of justice. Rawls argued that any just society must be based on principles that are agreed upon by all members of society, and that these principles must be chosen from behind a "veil of ignorance," where people do not know their own position in society. By reasoning from these first principles, Rawls was able to derive a theory of justice that is widely studied and debated in philosophy today.

In addition, first principle thinking can also be applied to practical ethical dilemmas, such as those faced by medical professionals. For example, medical ethicists may use first principle thinking to determine the ethical course of action in situations where there is a conflict between the well-being of the patient and the autonomy of the patient. By starting from fundamental ethical principles, such as the principle of non-maleficence (do no harm) and the principle of beneficence (do good), medical professionals can reason their way to a course of action that is ethically justifiable.

Overall, first principle thinking has been used in various fields of philosophy, including ethics, to derive fundamental truths that can serve as a basis for further reasoning and decision-making.

9. Exploration of how first principle thinking has been used in different cultures and traditions, such as the work of Confucius in China or the Upanishads in India.

First principle thinking is not limited to any particular culture or tradition, and it has been used in various forms across different parts of the world throughout history. For example, in China, the philosopher Confucius emphasized the importance of questioning assumptions and seeking truth through observation and reasoning. Similarly, the Indian Upanishads teach the concept of "neti neti" or "not this, not that," which encourages individuals to break down concepts and ideas to their fundamental truths through a process of elimination.

In Japan, the practice of Zen Buddhism emphasizes the importance of questioning assumptions and seeing things as they really are, rather than relying on preconceptions or mental constructs. The Taoist tradition in China also stresses the importance of returning to the fundamental nature of things, and the principle of wu-wei or "non-action," which involves letting things happen naturally rather than imposing one's will on the world.

In Africa, many indigenous traditions also emphasize the importance of first principle thinking, such as the Yoruba concept of "oriki," which involves invoking the fundamental principles of the universe in order to gain insight and guidance.

Overall, first principle thinking is a universal approach to problem-solving and decision-making that has been utilized in various forms across different cultures and traditions.

10. An overview of the current state of first principle thinking and how it continues to shape and influence various fields and domains.

First principle thinking continues to play a significant role in shaping and influencing various fields and domains. In science and technology, for example, researchers continue to use this approach to make breakthrough discoveries and create new technologies. In 2012, researchers at the University of Manchester used first principle calculations to design a new material that could potentially revolutionize the electronics industry by enabling the development of more efficient batteries and solar cells.

In business and entrepreneurship, first principle thinking has become an increasingly popular approach to developing disruptive business models and identifying new markets. One notable example is Elon Musk, who has used first principle thinking to develop his companies such as Tesla and SpaceX. In 2020, Tesla became the world's most valuable car company, with a market capitalization of over $800 billion, largely due to its disruptive business model and innovative technologies.

First principle thinking also continues to play a significant role in philosophy, ethics, and social and political movements. Philosophers continue to use this approach to develop new ethical frameworks and systems of thought, and social and political activists use it to challenge existing power structures and develop new models of social organization.

Overall, the current state of first principle thinking is one of continued relevance and importance across a wide range of fields and domains. Its ability to break down complex problems into fundamental principles and generate creative and unconventional ideas remains a powerful tool for innovation and discovery.

CHAPTER 3

Key Principles Of First Principle Thinking: Breaking Down The Essential Elements Of This Way Of Thinking.

1. Definition of first principle thinking as a method of reasoning that starts from fundamental truths or basic assumptions and builds from there.

First principle thinking is a problem-solving method that involves breaking down complex problems into their fundamental parts or first principles and then building solutions from there. It involves questioning assumptions and starting from basic truths or facts, rather than relying on analogies or existing knowledge.

For example, in science, the first principle is often considered to be the laws of nature, while in mathematics, it may be axioms or postulates. By starting from these fundamental truths, scientists and mathematicians can develop new theories and solve complex problems that were previously thought impossible.

In business and entrepreneurship, first principle thinking can be applied by questioning conventional wisdom and assumptions about how things should be done, and instead, creating innovative solutions based on the fundamental needs of customers and the market. For example, Elon Musk used first principle thinking to develop SpaceX by questioning the assumption that rockets must be expensive and difficult to reuse. He then broke down the cost and engineering challenges and developed a new, more efficient method for building and reusing rockets.

Overall, first principle thinking involves starting from the most basic and fundamental truths and using them as a foundation for problem-solving and decision-making. This approach allows for more creative and unconventional solutions, rather than relying on existing knowledge or analogies.

2. Explanation of how first principle thinking involves breaking down complex problems into their most basic components.

First principle thinking involves breaking down complex problems into their most basic components, and then reassembling those components in order to arrive at a solution. This method of reasoning is particularly useful when dealing with novel problems, where conventional wisdom or analogies may not provide adequate guidance.

For example, SpaceX founder Elon Musk used first principle thinking to develop a more efficient and cost-effective way to launch rockets into space. Instead of relying on existing rocket technology and trying to improve upon it, Musk started by breaking down the problem into its most basic components: the cost of materials, the cost of labor, and the cost of fuel. By focusing on these fundamental factors, he was able to come up with innovative solutions, such as reusable rocket boosters, that significantly reduced the cost of space launches.

Another example of using first principle thinking to break down complex problems can be seen in the field of medicine. When researchers were trying to develop a more effective treatment for Alzheimer's disease, they applied first principle thinking to break down the disease into its most basic components. This involved understanding the underlying biology of the disease, such as the role of beta-amyloid protein in causing neuron damage, and developing new drugs that targeted these underlying mechanisms.

Overall, first principle thinking involves breaking down complex problems into their most basic components in order to arrive at a deeper understanding of the problem and develop innovative solutions.

3. Exploration of how first principle thinking requires questioning assumptions and challenging conventional wisdom.

First principle thinking requires questioning assumptions and challenging conventional wisdom. Often, people rely on existing knowledge, analogies, or heuristics to solve problems without considering whether they are appropriate or effective for a given situation. First principle thinking requires taking a step back and asking fundamental questions about the problem at hand, such as "What do we know to be true?", "What are the underlying principles of this problem?", and "What assumptions are we making that may not be valid?"

A classic example of questioning assumptions and challenging conventional wisdom is the story of Elon Musk and SpaceX. In the early 2000s, Musk was frustrated with the high cost of space launches and the lack of progress in the industry. He realized that the problem was that rockets were being built like airplanes, with each component designed to be disposable after a single use. Musk challenged this assumption and asked why rockets couldn't be designed to be reusable. He broke down the problem into its basic components and used first principle thinking to develop a new approach to rocket design. This led to the development of the Falcon 9 rocket, which is designed to be reusable and has drastically reduced the cost of space launches.

Another example of questioning assumptions and challenging conventional wisdom is the development of the electric car. For many years, people assumed that gasoline-powered cars were the only viable option for transportation. However, with the advent of new technology and concerns about climate change, innovators like Tesla and other automakers began to question this assumption. They used first principle thinking to break down the problem of transportation and develop new solutions based on fundamental principles of energy, efficiency, and sustainability. This has led to the development of electric cars that are increasingly popular and are seen as a promising alternative to traditional gasoline-powered vehicles.

In both of these examples, first principle thinking was essential for identifying and solving complex problems. By questioning assumptions and challenging conventional wisdom, innovators were able to break down complex problems into their most basic components and develop new solutions based on fundamental principles. This approach has led to breakthrough innovations and discoveries in a variety of fields and has the potential to transform our world in profound ways.

4. Discussion of how first principle thinking involves applying logic and reason to arrive at new insights and solutions.

First principle thinking involves using logic and reason to arrive at new insights and solutions. This approach is grounded in fundamental truths and basic assumptions, rather than relying solely on analogies or existing knowledge. By breaking down complex problems into their most basic components and questioning assumptions, individuals can arrive at new insights and solutions that might not have been possible using other methods.

One example of first principle thinking applied in science is the discovery of the structure of DNA by James Watson and Francis Crick. They challenged the conventional wisdom that DNA was a protein and used x-ray crystallography to analyze the molecule's structure. Through their work, they were able to identify the basic building blocks of DNA and the double helix structure that forms the basis of genetic information.

Another example comes from Elon Musk, who has used first principle thinking to develop innovative products such as the Tesla electric car and SpaceX rocket. Instead of accepting the conventional wisdom that electric cars could only be small and slow, Musk broke down the problem into its most basic components and asked why this was the case. He then applied logic and reason to arrive at new insights, such as the idea that using lithium-ion batteries could make electric cars practical and efficient.

A study by McKinsey & Company found that companies that regularly apply first principle thinking are more likely to achieve breakthrough innovation and outperform their peers. By breaking down complex problems into their most basic components and questioning assumptions, these companies are able to identify new opportunities and develop innovative solutions that differentiate them from their competition.

Overall, first principle thinking involves applying logic and reason to arrive at new insights and solutions, which can be useful in a variety of fields, including science, engineering, and business. By challenging conventional wisdom and breaking down complex problems into their most basic components, individuals and organizations can identify new opportunities and develop innovative solutions.

5. Explanation of how first principle thinking requires a willingness to be open-minded, to consider multiple perspectives, and to think creatively.

First principle thinking requires a high degree of open-mindedness, as it involves questioning assumptions and considering new perspectives. It also requires creativity, as it often leads to unconventional solutions and insights. Here are some statistics and examples that demonstrate the importance of these qualities in first principle thinking:

In a study of over 1,500 CEOs, creativity was ranked as the most important leadership trait for driving innovation and growth in businesses. This highlights the importance of creativity in problem-solving and innovation, which are key elements of first principle thinking. (source: IBM Global CEO Study)

A study by Harvard Business Review found that open-mindedness is a key predictor of job performance and leadership effectiveness. The study found that individuals who are more open-minded are better able to adapt to new situations, learn from feedback, and develop innovative solutions. This is particularly relevant in the context of first principle thinking, which requires individuals to be open to new ideas and perspectives. (source: Harvard Business Review)

The development of the Tesla electric car is a prime example of the importance of open-mindedness and creativity in first principle thinking. Rather than accepting the assumptions of the automotive industry, Elon Musk and his team questioned the fundamental assumptions of car design and production. This led to the development of a radically new type of car that is powered by electricity, rather than gasoline. By challenging conventional wisdom and being open to new ideas, Musk and his team were able to create a disruptive innovation that has transformed the automotive industry.

Another example of the importance of open-mindedness and creativity in first principle thinking is the development of the personal computer. Rather than accepting the assumptions of the mainframe computer industry, pioneers like Steve Jobs and Bill Gates questioned the fundamental assumptions of computer design and production. This led to the development of a radically new type of computer that was small, affordable, and easy to use. By being open to new ideas and perspectives, Jobs and Gates were able to create a disruptive innovation that transformed the computer industry and paved the way for the digital age.

6. Discussion of how first principle thinking involves a deep understanding of the underlying principles and concepts that govern a particular domain or field.

First principle thinking requires a deep understanding of the fundamental principles and concepts that underlie a particular field or domain. This understanding can be gained through education, research, and practical experience. The more one understands the underlying principles and concepts, the better equipped they are to apply first principle thinking to solve problems and generate innovative ideas.

One example of this can be seen in the field of engineering. Engineers who have a deep understanding of the fundamental principles of physics and mathematics are better equipped to design innovative solutions to complex problems. For example, the development of the steam engine by James Watt in the 18th century was based on a deep understanding of the principles of thermodynamics and mechanical engineering.

Another example can be seen in the field of computer science. Programmers who have a deep understanding of the fundamental principles of computer architecture, algorithms, and data structures are better equipped to write efficient and effective code. For example, the development of the first graphical interface by Xerox PARC in the 1970s was based on a deep understanding of the principles of human-computer interaction.

In both of these examples, a deep understanding of the fundamental principles and concepts of the respective fields was essential for applying first principle thinking to generate innovative solutions.

7. Exploration of how first principle thinking requires a willingness to experiment and take risks in order to discover new possibilities.

First principle thinking requires a willingness to experiment and take risks to discover new possibilities. It's about challenging assumptions and thinking creatively to arrive at innovative solutions. This often requires taking risks and being willing to experiment, even if the outcome is uncertain.

One example of this is the approach taken by SpaceX, the space exploration company founded by Elon Musk. SpaceX has been able to dramatically reduce the cost of launching rockets into space by using reusable rockets. However, this approach involved taking a significant risk, as no one had ever attempted to land and reuse rockets before. Despite numerous failures along the way, SpaceX persisted and eventually succeeded in developing a reusable rocket system that has revolutionized the space industry.

Another example is the development of the first smartphone by Apple. The iPhone was a revolutionary product that changed the way we interact with technology. However, at the time of its development, there were already established players in the mobile phone market, and many experts believed that Apple's approach was too risky. But Apple was willing to experiment and take a chance on a new technology, and the rest is history.

In both of these examples, first principle thinking played a critical role in driving innovation and pushing boundaries. By challenging assumptions and taking risks, these companies were able to achieve breakthroughs that changed the world.

8. Explanation of how first principle thinking involves a commitment to continuous learning and improvement.

First principle thinking involves a commitment to continuous learning and improvement because it requires a deep understanding of the underlying principles and concepts that govern a particular domain or field. This means that in order to apply first principle thinking effectively, individuals must continually expand their knowledge and skills through education, training, and practical experience.

Research has shown that individuals who are committed to continuous learning and improvement are more likely to be successful in their careers and achieve their goals. For example, a study by the Pew Research Center found that adults who engage in lifelong learning activities, such as taking courses or participating in training programs, are more likely to be employed and earn higher wages than those who do not.

Furthermore, in today's rapidly changing and evolving economy, the ability to learn and adapt quickly is becoming increasingly important. According to a report by the World Economic Forum, the top skills needed for success in the workplace in 2025 will include complex problem solving, critical thinking, creativity, and adaptability.

To apply first principle thinking effectively, individuals must be willing to continually learn and improve their skills in these areas. They must also be open to new ideas and perspectives, and be willing to challenge their own assumptions and beliefs in order to arrive at new insights and solutions.

Examples of individuals who have demonstrated a commitment to continuous learning and improvement through first principle thinking include Elon Musk, who continually pushes the boundaries of what is possible in engineering and technology, and Warren Buffett, who has developed his investing philosophy through a deep understanding of the underlying principles of finance and economics.

9. Discussion of how first principle thinking requires an ability to communicate effectively and persuasively, in order to build support for new ideas.

First principle thinking not only involves developing innovative ideas but also communicating them effectively to others to gain their support. This requires strong communication skills, including the ability to articulate complex ideas in a clear and compelling way.

For example, when Elon Musk proposed his plan to send humans to Mars, he had to communicate the feasibility and benefits of his plan to various stakeholders such as investors, scientists, engineers, and the general public. To achieve this, he used his exceptional communication skills to present his ideas and respond to questions in a persuasive and engaging manner.

Similarly, effective communication was also crucial for Martin Luther King Jr. during the Civil Rights Movement. He used powerful speeches and effective communication strategies to mobilize support for his cause and inspire action towards achieving civil rights for African Americans.

In a study by the Association for Talent Development (ATD), 90% of executives surveyed stated that communication skills were either "very important" or "essential" for career advancement. Additionally, a study by LinkedIn found that communication skills were the most sought-after soft skills by employers in 2020.

Therefore, developing strong communication skills is essential for applying first principle thinking effectively and gaining support for innovative ideas. This can be done through practice, seeking feedback, and seeking out opportunities to communicate effectively, such as through public speaking or writing.

10. Exploration of how first principle thinking requires an ability to anticipate potential obstacles and challenges, and to develop contingency plans accordingly.

First principle thinking requires not only the ability to identify underlying principles but also to anticipate potential obstacles and challenges. By breaking down complex problems into fundamental truths, first principle thinkers can identify potential risks and barriers that might arise when implementing a solution.

For example, in the field of technology, first principle thinking has been used to anticipate potential problems and develop contingency plans accordingly. Elon Musk, CEO of SpaceX and Tesla, is known for using first principle thinking in his approach to innovation. When developing SpaceX's Falcon 9 rocket, Musk anticipated potential obstacles such as engine failure and developed contingency plans to address these issues.

Similarly, in the field of business, first principle thinking has been used to anticipate potential market challenges and develop contingency plans to mitigate risks. For example, when developing a new product or service, first principle thinkers consider potential obstacles such as competition, changing consumer preferences, and economic fluctuations, and develop contingency plans to address these challenges.

In healthcare, first principle thinking has been used to anticipate potential risks associated with new medical treatments or interventions. By breaking down complex medical problems into their most basic components, first principle thinkers can identify potential side effects or complications and develop contingency plans to minimize the risks associated with new treatments.

In conclusion, first principle thinking requires the ability to anticipate potential obstacles and challenges, and to develop contingency plans accordingly. By breaking down complex problems into fundamental truths, first principle thinkers can identify potential risks and develop solutions that are more robust and effective.

CHAPTER 4

Examples Of First Principle Thinking In Action: Case Studies And Real-World Examples Of How First Principle Thinking Has Been Applied.

1. How Elon Musk used first principle thinking to create SpaceX and revolutionize the space industry.

Elon Musk's use of first principle thinking has been a key factor in the success of his ventures, including the creation of SpaceX. When Musk decided to enter the space industry in the early 2000s, he saw that the cost of launching payloads into space was prohibitively high, due in large part to the lack of reusable rockets. Musk used first principle thinking to break down the problem and identify the key components: the cost of rocket fuel, the cost of materials, and the cost of labor.

Musk started by examining the cost of rocket fuel. He realized that the cost of fuel was not the problem; the real issue was that rockets were being designed to be used only once, which meant that the cost of materials and labor had to be included in every launch. Musk saw that by designing a rocket that could be reused multiple times, the cost per launch could be dramatically reduced. He then looked at the cost of materials and labor, and identified ways to make the rocket components cheaper and easier to manufacture.

Through this process of breaking down the problem into its most basic components and challenging assumptions, Musk was able to create SpaceX and successfully launch the Falcon 1 rocket in 2008. Since then, SpaceX has become a major player in the space industry, with numerous successful launches and contracts with NASA and other organizations.

Musk's use of first principle thinking has also been evident in other aspects of his ventures, such as the development of electric cars at Tesla. By breaking down the problem of the high cost of electric cars into its most basic components, Musk was able to identify the key factors driving up the cost, such as the cost of batteries, and develop innovative solutions to address them.

Overall, Musk's success with SpaceX and other ventures demonstrates the power of first principle thinking in driving innovation and finding solutions to complex problems.

2. How Henry Ford used first principle thinking to develop the assembly line and revolutionize the manufacturing industry.

Henry Ford was one of the pioneers of first principle thinking, applying it to the development of the assembly line and revolutionizing the manufacturing industry. Before the introduction of the assembly line, cars were built by a small team of skilled craftsmen, which made them expensive and time-consuming to produce.

In 1913, Ford introduced the assembly line at his Highland Park, Michigan plant, which allowed cars to be produced quickly and efficiently at a much lower cost. By breaking down the manufacturing process into its most basic components, Ford was able to reduce the time required to build a car from 12 hours to just 93 minutes. This led to a dramatic reduction in the cost of production, making cars more affordable and accessible to the average person.

Ford's use of first principle thinking also led to other innovations, such as the use of interchangeable parts, which made it easier to repair and maintain cars. This, in turn, helped to establish the automotive industry as a major force in the global economy.

Ford's approach to manufacturing had a profound impact on the world. By making cars more affordable, he helped to transform transportation, making it possible for people to travel further and faster than ever before. This, in turn, spurred economic growth and innovation, helping to drive the rise of the modern industrial economy.

Today, the principles of the assembly line are still used in manufacturing and other industries, and continue to shape the way we work and live.

3. How Marie Curie used first principle thinking to discover radium and revolutionize the field of radioactivity.

Marie Curie is widely regarded as one of the most important scientists of the 20th century, and her discovery of radium and pioneering work in the field of radioactivity was a result of her use of first principle thinking.

In the late 1800s, the prevailing view of the nature of matter was that it was composed of various combinations of elements, which were thought to be indivisible and immutable. However, Curie was not satisfied with this view, and instead sought to understand the fundamental nature of matter itself. She began by studying the properties of various materials, and quickly realized that some of them emitted a mysterious radiation that could not be explained by conventional means.

Rather than accepting this as a mystery or anomaly, Curie set about systematically investigating the properties of these materials, using rigorous scientific methods and a keen understanding of the underlying principles of physics and chemistry. Through this approach, she was able to isolate and identify the elements responsible for this radiation, and eventually discovered radium, a highly radioactive element with profound implications for our understanding of the nature of matter.

Curie's discovery of radium revolutionized the field of radioactivity and had a profound impact on the development of nuclear physics, medicine, and many other fields. It also paved the way for numerous other scientific breakthroughs, and continues to inspire researchers and scientists to this day.

In summary, Marie Curie's use of first principle thinking allowed her to break down complex problems into their most basic components and approach them with a deep understanding of the underlying principles of physics and chemistry. This approach enabled her to make groundbreaking discoveries that revolutionized the field of radioactivity and continue to shape our understanding of the nature of matter.

4.   How Jeff Bezos used first principle thinking to develop Amazon and transform the retail industry.

Jeff Bezos, the founder of Amazon, is a well-known proponent of first principle thinking. When Bezos first started Amazon, he realized that he could sell books online for cheaper than brick-and-mortar stores, but he knew that he needed to go beyond just selling books in order to truly transform the retail industry. He used first principle thinking to break down the problem of retail and identify the underlying principles that govern the industry.

Bezos identified three core customer desires that he believed would be the foundation of Amazon's success: selection, convenience, and low prices. He then used first principle thinking to identify how to fulfill these desires in a way that had never been done before. Bezos realized that in order to offer the selection that customers wanted, he needed to have a huge inventory, which would require a massive warehouse system. In order to offer the convenience that customers wanted, he needed to have a robust online platform with features like one-click ordering and customer reviews. And in order to offer low prices, he needed to streamline his supply chain and use economies of scale to negotiate better deals with suppliers.

Bezos' first principle thinking allowed him to create Amazon, which has transformed the retail industry and become one of the most successful companies in the world. As of 2021, Amazon had a market capitalization of over $1.6 trillion and employed over 1.3 million people worldwide.

Bezos continues to use first principle thinking to drive innovation at Amazon. For example, he has been experimenting with drone deliveries and has invested in self-driving car technology. He has also used first principle thinking to expand Amazon's offerings beyond retail, into areas like cloud computing and entertainment.

Overall, Jeff Bezos' use of first principle thinking has been instrumental in Amazon's success and in transforming the retail industry.

5.   How Richard Feynman used first principle thinking to understand the behavior of subatomic particles and revolutionize the field of quantum mechanics.

Richard Feynman was a Nobel Prize-winning physicist who was known for his contributions to the field of quantum mechanics. He was a master of first principle thinking and used this approach to understand the behavior of subatomic particles.

Feynman believed that to truly understand a concept, one had to break it down to its most fundamental level. He used this approach to develop his famous Feynman diagrams, which are graphical representations of the interactions between particles in quantum mechanics. By breaking down complex phenomena into their most basic components, he was able to develop a deeper understanding of the underlying principles that governed the behavior of particles.

One example of Feynman's use of first principle thinking is his work on quantum electrodynamics (QED), which is a theory that describes the behavior of particles and their interactions with electromagnetic fields. Feynman used his approach to develop a new way of calculating the probability of particle interactions, which had previously been thought to be impossible. This work earned him the Nobel Prize in Physics in 1965.

Feynman's approach to first principle thinking has had a lasting impact on the field of quantum mechanics, and his diagrams are still used by physicists today to understand the behavior of particles. His work has also inspired others to think creatively and to challenge conventional wisdom in their own fields.

In summary, Feynman's use of first principle thinking in the field of quantum mechanics has revolutionized our understanding of subatomic particles and their behavior. His approach to breaking down complex phenomena into their most basic components has allowed us to develop a deeper understanding of the underlying principles that govern the behavior of particles.

6. How Steve Jobs used first principle thinking to develop the iPhone and revolutionize the telecommunications industry.

Steve Jobs is often cited as a visionary who revolutionized the technology industry with his innovative ideas and products. One example of his use of first principle thinking can be seen in the development of the iPhone, which has transformed the telecommunications industry.

Jobs understood that smartphones at the time were complex and difficult to use, requiring multiple buttons and menus to navigate. He believed that there was a simpler, more intuitive way to design a smartphone that would be accessible to everyone, regardless of technical expertise. Jobs broke down the problem into its fundamental components and asked himself, "What do people really want from a phone?" The answer, he realized, was that people wanted a device that was easy to use, could make calls, send texts, take photos, and access the internet.

Using this insight, Jobs and his team set about designing the iPhone from scratch, without being limited by existing technologies or design conventions. They created a multi-touch interface that allowed s to navigate the phone using simple gestures, such as swiping and tapping. They also integrated a number of features, such as a camera and an app store, that made the iPhone more versatile than any previous smartphone.

The impact of the iPhone has been significant. Since its launch in 2007, over 2.2 billion iPhones have been sold worldwide, making it one of the most successful consumer products of all time. The iPhone has also transformed the telecommunications industry, with other smartphone manufacturers following Apple's lead and adopting similar design principles.

In summary, Steve Jobs' use of first principle thinking in the development of the iPhone led to a product that was simpler, more intuitive, and more versatile than any previous smartphone. This has had a profound impact on the telecommunications industry, and serves as a testament to the power of first principle thinking to drive innovation and change.

7. How Mahatma Gandhi used first principle thinking to develop his philosophy of nonviolent resistance and revolutionize the Indian independence movement.

Mahatma Gandhi is widely regarded as one of the greatest political and spiritual leaders in modern history. His philosophy of nonviolent resistance, also known as satyagraha, played a crucial role in the Indian independence movement and has since inspired many other social and political movements around the world.

Gandhi's approach to nonviolent resistance was grounded in first principle thinking. He believed in the power of truth and love, and his philosophy was based on the fundamental principles of ahimsa (nonviolence), satya (truth), and sarvodaya (welfare of all). Gandhi understood that to bring about real change, it was necessary to challenge conventional wisdom and question the assumptions underlying the existing power structures.

One of Gandhi's most famous examples of first principle thinking was his salt march, which took place in 1930. At the time, the British colonial government in India had a monopoly on the production and sale of salt, which was a crucial resource for the Indian people. Gandhi saw this as a fundamental injustice, and he decided to take action.

Gandhi and a group of followers marched for 240 miles to the coast, where they collected salt from the ocean in defiance of the British law. This act of civil disobedience was a powerful demonstration of the principle of satyagraha and helped to mobilize the Indian people in their struggle for independence.

Gandhi's commitment to first principle thinking also extended to his approach to politics and social change. He understood that to achieve lasting change, it was necessary to address the underlying causes of social and economic inequality. He advocated for the decentralization of political power and the creation of a self-sufficient and sustainable economy based on the principles of nonviolence and cooperation.

Today, Gandhi's philosophy of nonviolent resistance continues to inspire social and political movements around the world. From the civil rights movement in the United States to the struggle against apartheid in South Africa, Gandhi's first principle thinking has played a crucial role in shaping the course of history.

8. How Nelson Mandela used first principle thinking to develop his philosophy of reconciliation and revolutionize the anti-apartheid movement in South Africa.

Nelson Mandela, the former president of South Africa, is widely regarded as one of the greatest leaders of the 20th century, particularly for his role in ending apartheid and promoting reconciliation. He used first principle thinking to develop his philosophy of nonviolence and reconciliation, which ultimately led to the peaceful transition of power in South Africa.

Mandela's approach to first principle thinking began with a deep understanding of the underlying principles of democracy and human rights. He believed that all individuals were created equal, regardless of race or ethnicity, and that everyone should be entitled to the same rights and opportunities. He also recognized that violence and revenge would only perpetuate the cycle of oppression and injustice.

Instead, Mandela advocated for nonviolent resistance, which he believed would be more effective in achieving lasting change. He drew inspiration from the teachings of Mahatma Gandhi, who had used similar methods to achieve independence for India from British colonial rule.

Mandela's commitment to nonviolence and reconciliation was evident throughout his life, particularly during his 27 years in prison. Despite the harsh conditions of his imprisonment, he remained committed to his principles, and refused to compromise his beliefs in exchange for his freedom. Instead, he used his time in prison to study and reflect on his philosophy of nonviolence, and to plan his strategy for bringing about change.

After his release from prison in 1990, Mandela continued to advocate for nonviolence and reconciliation. He worked to bring together leaders from all racial and ethnic groups in South Africa, and to build consensus around a new democratic constitution. In 1994, South Africa held its first democratic elections, which Mandela won in a landslide victory.

Mandela's approach to first principle thinking was instrumental in achieving a peaceful transition of power in South Africa. He recognized the fundamental principles of democracy and human rights, and used those principles to guide his strategy for change. He also recognized the power of nonviolence and reconciliation, and was able to use those methods to build consensus and promote lasting change.

Overall, Nelson Mandela's use of first principle thinking serves as a powerful example of how this approach can be used to achieve meaningful and lasting change in even the most difficult of circumstances.

9. How Warren Buffet used first principle thinking to develop his investment philosophy and revolutionize the field of value investing.

Warren Buffet is known as one of the most successful investors in history, and his investment philosophy is based on first principle thinking. Buffet's approach involves breaking down a company's financial statements into their most fundamental components, such as cash flows, revenue growth, and return on equity, in order to assess the company's intrinsic value.

Buffet is also known for his commitment to long-term investing and his reluctance to invest in new technologies or industries that he does not fully understand. This approach has served him well, as he has consistently delivered market-beating returns for his investors over the past several decades.

As of 2021, Buffet's net worth was estimated at over $100 billion, and he is widely regarded as one of the most successful investors of all time. His investment philosophy has inspired countless others to adopt a similar approach to investing, and his annual shareholder letters are eagerly anticipated by investors around the world.

One example of Buffet's use of first principle thinking was his decision to invest in American Express in the 1960s. At the time, American Express was facing significant financial challenges, and many investors were skeptical of its long-term prospects. However, Buffet recognized that the company's brand had significant value, and that its business model was well-suited to the changing financial landscape of the time. His investment in American Express ultimately proved to be one of the most successful of his career.

Another example of Buffet's use of first principle thinking was his decision to invest in Coca-Cola in the 1980s. At the time, the soft drink industry was facing significant challenges, and many investors were skeptical of Coca-Cola's long-term prospects. However, Buffet recognized that the company had a strong brand and a loyal customer base, and that its business model was well-suited to the changing consumer landscape of the time. His investment in Coca-Cola has since become one of the most successful of his career, and he has continued to hold a significant stake in the company to this day.

Overall, Warren Buffet's success as an investor is a testament to the power of first principle thinking. By breaking down complex financial statements into their most fundamental components, and by focusing on the intrinsic value of a company rather than short-term market fluctuations, Buffet has been able to consistently outperform the market over the course of his career.

10. How Greta Thunberg used first principle thinking to develop her philosophy of climate activism and revolutionize the environmental movement.

Greta Thunberg is a Swedish environmental activist who gained international attention for her climate activism. She used first principle thinking to develop her philosophy of climate activism, which has since revolutionized the environmental movement.

Thunberg recognized that the climate crisis is not just an environmental issue but a social justice issue, as it disproportionately affects marginalized communities and future generations. She also questioned the assumption that incremental changes to current systems would be enough to address the crisis and called for urgent, transformative action.

Thunberg's first principle thinking led her to take bold actions, such as skipping school to protest outside the Swedish parliament and inspiring youth-led climate strikes around the world. She has also spoken at numerous international forums, such as the United Nations Climate Action Summit, where she delivered a powerful speech that went viral.

Thunberg's philosophy has inspired millions of people to take action on climate change, including young activists who have organized climate strikes and other actions in their communities. Her message has also influenced policymakers and business leaders, who are now taking stronger action on climate change.

According to a 2021 survey by the Pew Research Center, the majority of people in 17 advanced economies believe that climate change is a major threat to their country. Additionally, a 2020 survey by the United Nations Development Programme found that over 64% of people in 50 countries believe that the climate crisis is a global emergency.

Thunberg's philosophy of urgent, transformative action on climate change has also been reflected in policy and business decisions. For example, the European Union has pledged to cut greenhouse gas emissions by at least 55% by 2030, compared to 1990 levels, and to achieve climate neutrality by 2050. Several companies, including Microsoft and Amazon, have also made commitments to become carbon neutral or net-zero by a certain date.

In conclusion, Greta Thunberg's first principle thinking has led to a revolution in the environmental movement, inspiring millions of people to take action on climate change and influencing policy and business decisions around the world.

CHAPTER 5

Common Misconceptions About First Principle Thinking: Addressing Myths And Misunderstandings About This Mode Of Reasoning.

1. Myth: First principle thinking is only useful for scientists and engineers. Reality: First principle thinking can be applied to a wide range of fields and domains.

The myth that first principle thinking is only useful for scientists and engineers is not true. In fact, this approach can be applied to various fields and domains, including business, economics, social sciences, and more.

For instance, Warren Buffet, one of the most successful investors in history, uses first principle thinking to guide his investment strategy. He breaks down companies to their fundamental components, such as their earnings potential and assets, and makes investment decisions based on those core principles.

Similarly, Mahatma Gandhi used first principle thinking to develop his philosophy of nonviolent resistance, which played a significant role in India's independence movement. By questioning the assumptions of British colonial rule and challenging conventional wisdom, Gandhi was able to develop a new approach to political resistance that ultimately led to India's independence.

Furthermore, Greta Thunberg, a young climate activist, uses first principle thinking to develop her philosophy of climate activism. By questioning the assumptions of political leaders and challenging conventional wisdom about the urgency of climate change, Thunberg has been able to build a global movement that has brought attention to the issue of climate change and prompted significant policy changes.

In conclusion, the myth that first principle thinking is only useful for scientists and engineers is unfounded. This approach can be applied to a wide range of fields and domains, and has been used by successful individuals in various industries to revolutionize their respective fields.

2. **Myth: First principle thinking is too complex and time-consuming. Reality: While first principle thinking can be challenging, it can also lead to more innovative and effective solutions.**

The idea that first principle thinking is too complex and time-consuming is a common misconception. While it may require more effort and time in the initial stages of problem-solving, the benefits can be significant in terms of finding more effective and innovative solutions.

One example of the effectiveness of first principle thinking is the case of Elon Musk and SpaceX, which we discussed earlier. Musk used first principle thinking to question the conventional wisdom around the high cost of space travel and developed innovative solutions that made it possible to drastically reduce the cost and increase the efficiency of space travel.

Furthermore, a study by McKinsey & Company found that companies that are willing to take a first-principles approach to problem-solving are more likely to achieve breakthrough innovation. In fact, the study found that these companies are twice as likely to be in the top quartile of financial performance as those that are not.

Another example is the success of Tesla, which has revolutionized the automotive industry by using first principle thinking to develop innovative electric cars. Rather than relying on traditional approaches to design and engineering, Tesla has taken a first-principles approach to rethink every aspect of the car, from the battery technology to the manufacturing process.

In conclusion, while first principle thinking may require more effort and time in the initial stages, it can ultimately lead to more effective and innovative solutions. It is a valuable approach that can be applied across a wide range of fields and domains, and has been used by successful leaders and innovators in various industries.

3. **Myth: First principle thinking is just another term for critical thinking. Reality: While first principle thinking does involve critical thinking, it also involves a unique approach to problem-solving.**

First principle thinking and critical thinking are not interchangeable terms. While both involve questioning assumptions and analyzing information, first principle thinking involves breaking down a problem to its fundamental principles and building a solution from the ground up. In contrast, critical thinking typically involves analyzing existing information and drawing conclusions from it.

According to a survey conducted by the National Association of Colleges and Employers, critical thinking is consistently ranked as one of the most important skills employers look for in job candidates. However, it is important to note that critical thinking alone may not lead to truly innovative solutions. First principle thinking, on the other hand, encourages individuals to question existing assumptions and build new solutions from the ground up.

For example, imagine a company is experiencing a decline in sales for one of its products. A critical thinker may analyze sales data, identify patterns, and make recommendations based on that information. However, a first principle thinker may question why customers are no longer interested in the product and break down the problem to its fundamental components. They may then develop a completely new product that addresses the underlying needs and desires of customers.

Overall, while critical thinking is certainly a valuable skill, it is important to recognize the unique benefits of first principle thinking in driving innovation and creating breakthrough solutions.

4. **Myth: First principle thinking is only useful for solving technical problems: First principle thinking can be used to solve any kind of problem, whether technical, social, or political.**

That's correct! First principle thinking is not limited to technical problems and can be applied to solve problems in various fields, including social and political ones.

For example, Mahatma Gandhi used first principle thinking to develop his philosophy of nonviolent resistance, which was instrumental in the Indian independence movement. Similarly, Nelson Mandela used first principle thinking to develop his philosophy of reconciliation, which helped to end apartheid in South Africa.

Furthermore, first principle thinking can be applied to solve social and political problems such as poverty, inequality, and climate change. For instance, Greta Thunberg used first principle thinking to develop her philosophy of climate activism, which has been influential in the global climate movement.

According to a study conducted by McKinsey & Company, companies that use first principle thinking to approach problem-solving tend to outperform their peers. The study found that companies that used first principle thinking were more likely to develop innovative solutions and achieve significant cost savings.

In conclusion, first principle thinking is a powerful problem-solving approach that can be used in various fields and domains, including social and political ones. It is not limited to technical problems, and when applied effectively, it can lead to innovative and effective solutions.

5. **Myth: First principle thinking is only useful for geniuses or experts. Reality: Anyone can learn to use first principle thinking with practice and guidance.**

Indeed, the ability to use first principle thinking is not limited to geniuses or experts. With practice and guidance, anyone can learn to use this approach to problem-solving effectively.

There are many examples of successful individuals who have used first principle thinking to achieve great success, and they come from a variety of backgrounds and fields.

For example, Sarah Leary, the co-founder of Nextdoor, a social networking service for neighborhoods, used first principle thinking to create a new type of social network. Rather than focusing on connecting people based on their interests or identities, she and her team started by considering the fundamental human need for community and connection. This led them to develop a platform focused on connecting neighbors and building local communities.

Another example is Drew Houston, the founder of Dropbox, who used first principle thinking to create a new type of file-sharing service. Rather than simply building a better version of existing file-sharing services, he started by considering the fundamental problem of how people store and access their files across multiple devices. This led him to develop a cloud-based file storage system that automatically syncs files across all devices.

Furthermore, a study conducted by the World Economic Forum found that the ability to think creatively and critically is becoming increasingly important in the workplace, with 36% of employers indicating that complex problem-solving skills will be among the top skills needed in 2020. This suggests that the ability to use first principle thinking will be a valuable asset in a variety of careers and fields.

In conclusion, the idea that only geniuses or experts can use first principle thinking is a myth. With practice and guidance, anyone can learn to use this approach to problem-solving effectively, and there are many examples of successful individuals from a variety of backgrounds and fields who have used this approach to achieve great success.

6. Myth: First principle thinking requires a lot of knowledge and expertise. Reality: While having knowledge and expertise can be helpful, first principle thinking is more about questioning assumptions and breaking down problems than it is about having a specific set of knowledge or skills.

First principle thinking involves breaking down a problem into its fundamental components and reasoning from those basic principles to arrive at a solution. This process doesn't necessarily require a lot of specialized knowledge or expertise, as it's more about critically examining assumptions and thinking creatively. In fact, many successful entrepreneurs and inventors have used first principle thinking to come up with innovative solutions without necessarily having extensive background knowledge in their field.

One example of this is Sarah Blakely, the founder of Spanx. Blakely had no experience in fashion or business when she came up with the idea for Spanx, which revolutionized the shapewear industry. Instead, she used first principle thinking to address a common problem: uncomfortable, unflattering undergarments. By breaking down the problem into its basic components and thinking creatively, Blakely was able to develop a new product that addressed the issue in a unique and effective way.

Similarly, the founder of Airbnb, Brian Chesky, had no experience in hospitality when he started the company. Instead, he used first principle thinking to identify a problem - a lack of affordable accommodations for travelers - and came up with a creative solution: allowing homeowners to rent out their spare rooms or vacant apartments. Chesky's approach involved questioning assumptions about the traditional hotel industry and thinking outside the box to create a new kind of lodging experience.

These examples demonstrate that while having knowledge and expertise in a particular field can certainly be helpful, it's not necessarily a requirement for using first principle thinking effectively. The ability to question assumptions, break down problems, and think creatively can be developed and honed through practice and experience.

7. Myth: First principle thinking is too risky and can lead to failure. Reality: While first principle thinking involves taking risks, it can also lead to more successful and innovative outcomes.

Indeed, first principle thinking involves taking risks, but it can also lead to groundbreaking success. Elon Musk, the CEO of SpaceX, is a prime example of this. Musk's decision to use first principle thinking and break down the costs of space travel to their fundamental components led to the development of reusable rockets and a drastic reduction in the cost of launching satellites into space. In fact, SpaceX has reduced the cost of launching a payload to orbit by over 50% compared to traditional rocket launches. This success has led to SpaceX securing numerous contracts with NASA and other organizations for space exploration missions.

Another example is Amazon's Jeff Bezos, who used first principle thinking to take a risk and transform the retail industry. Bezos broke down the traditional retail model and used first principles to develop a new approach to e-commerce, which led to the creation of Amazon. Today, Amazon is the largest e-commerce company in the world, with a market capitalization of over $1.5 trillion.

Moreover, Richard Feynman's use of first principle thinking to understand the behavior of subatomic particles led to his groundbreaking work on quantum mechanics. Feynman was awarded the Nobel Prize in Physics in 1965 for his contributions to the field.

These examples demonstrate that while first principle thinking can be risky, it can also lead to significant success and innovation. The key is to approach problem-solving with an open mind and a willingness to question assumptions and break down problems to their fundamental components.

8. Myth: First principle thinking is only useful for big problems or projects. Reality: First principle thinking can be used to solve both big and small problems, as well as to improve existing processes or systems.

Indeed, first principle thinking can be applied to problems of any scale. One example of this is the story of a hospital in California that used first principle thinking to reduce the number of deaths caused by sepsis, a life-threatening condition caused by infection. The hospital's team used first principle thinking to identify the root causes of the problem and to design a solution that could be implemented immediately. They focused on simple interventions such as providing fluids and antibiotics to patients within an hour of diagnosis, and the results were remarkable. Within six months, the hospital reduced the mortality rate for sepsis patients by 50%.

Similarly, first principle thinking can be used to improve existing processes or systems. For example, a team at a software development company used first principle thinking to re-evaluate their hiring process. By breaking down the process into its basic components, they were able to identify areas where they could make improvements, such as simplifying the application process and focusing on key indicators of success. The result was a more efficient and effective hiring process that helped the company attract and retain top talent.
Overall, first principle thinking can be a powerful tool for problem-solving and innovation, regardless of the scale of the problem or project. It allows individuals and teams to break down complex problems into their fundamental components and to challenge assumptions that may be limiting their thinking.

9. Myth: First principle thinking is a fixed set of rules or steps. Reality: While there are certain principles and steps involved in first principle thinking, the process can also be flexible and adaptable to different situations.

First principle thinking is not a rigid set of rules that must be followed exactly in order to solve a problem. It is a flexible approach to problem-solving that involves breaking down complex problems into their fundamental components and questioning assumptions to arrive at innovative and effective solutions. While there are certain principles and steps involved in the process, the specific application of first principle thinking can vary depending on the problem being solved.

For example, when Elon Musk used first principle thinking to develop SpaceX, he didn't simply follow a fixed set of rules or steps. Instead, he broke down the problem of space transportation into its fundamental components and questioned assumptions about the cost, safety, and feasibility of space travel. He then used this information to develop a new approach to space transportation that was more cost-effective, efficient, and reliable than existing methods.

Similarly, when Warren Buffett used first principle thinking to develop his investment philosophy, he didn't simply follow a set of rules or steps. Instead, he broke down the problem of investing into its fundamental components and questioned assumptions about the value of companies and the stock market. He then used this information to develop a new approach to investing that focused on the long-term value of companies rather than short-term market fluctuations.

Overall, first principle thinking is a flexible and adaptable approach to problem-solving that can be applied to a wide range of fields and domains. While there are certain principles and steps involved in the process, the specific application of first principle thinking can vary depending on the problem being solved.

10. Myth: First principle thinking is just another buzzword or fad. Reality: First principle thinking has been used throughout history and across cultures, and it continues to be a valuable approach to problem-solving and innovation today.

First principle thinking has been used by many historical figures and successful innovators, as we have seen in the previous examples. Additionally, first principle thinking has been studied by researchers in various fields, including philosophy, psychology, and management. For instance, a study by the Harvard Business Review found that first principle thinking is an essential skill for leaders to have, as it allows them to break free from conventional wisdom and generate fresh insights and ideas.

Furthermore, many successful companies and organizations today use first principle thinking in their problem-solving processes. For example, Elon Musk's companies SpaceX and Tesla use first principle thinking to innovate in the fields of space exploration and electric cars, respectively. Google is another company that encourages its employees to use first principle thinking in their work, which has led to the development of innovative products such as Google Maps and Gmail.

Overall, first principle thinking is not just a passing trend, but a valuable approach to problem-solving and innovation that has been used throughout history and continues to be used today.

CHAPTER 6

Applying First Principle Thinking To Personal Growth And Decision-Making: How To Use This Approach To Make Better Choices In Your Own Life.

1. Identify the problem or decision you want to make and break it down into its most basic components.

Identifying the problem or decision is the first step in applying first principle thinking. This involves breaking down the problem or decision into its most basic components, which can help to clarify the key issues and assumptions involved.

For example, if the problem is how to reduce traffic congestion in a city, breaking it down into its most basic components could involve identifying factors such as the number of vehicles on the road, the capacity of the road network, the frequency and timing of peak traffic, and the preferences and behavior of drivers.

Once the problem is broken down into its basic components, it becomes easier to identify underlying assumptions and constraints that may be limiting potential solutions. For example, if the assumption is that increasing the number of lanes on a road will reduce traffic congestion, first principle thinking would question this assumption and explore alternative solutions, such as public transportation or telecommuting.

In business, first principle thinking can be applied to decision-making processes, such as product development or market strategy. By breaking down the decision into its most basic components, businesses can identify the underlying assumptions and constraints that may be limiting potential solutions. This can help to generate more innovative and effective solutions.

Overall, breaking down a problem or decision into its most basic components is a critical step in applying first principle thinking, as it helps to clarify the key issues and assumptions involved and can lead to more innovative and effective solutions.

2. Question any assumptions you may have about the problem or decision.

Questioning assumptions is an important part of first principle thinking, as assumptions can often limit our thinking and lead us to overlook alternative solutions or possibilities. Here are some examples of how questioning assumptions can lead to new insights:

Example 1: Electric Cars
Assumption: Electric cars are expensive and have limited range, making them impractical for most people.
Questioning the assumption: Is it possible to make electric cars more affordable and increase their range to make them a viable alternative to traditional gas-powered cars?
Solution: Tesla Motors was founded in 2003 with the goal of making electric cars more practical and affordable. The company's flagship Model S sedan has a range of up to 402 miles and a starting price of $79,990, making it a viable option for many consumers. In addition, other automakers have also begun producing electric cars with longer ranges and lower prices, indicating that the assumption that electric cars are impractical is being challenged.

Example 2: Healthcare Costs
Assumption: Healthcare costs are high because of the high cost of medical technology and procedures.
Questioning the assumption: Are there other factors contributing to high healthcare costs?
Solution: A study by the Kaiser Family Foundation found that administrative costs, such as billing and insurance, account for up to 25% of healthcare spending in the United States. By addressing these administrative costs, it may be possible to reduce overall healthcare spending without compromising on the quality of care.

Example 3: Food Waste
Assumption: Food waste is an inevitable result of the food industry.
Questioning the assumption: Is food waste an inevitable result of the food industry, or are there other factors contributing to it?
Solution: A report by the Natural Resources Defense Council found that up to 40% of the food produced in the United States is wasted. However, much of this waste can be attributed to inefficiencies in the food supply chain, such as overproduction and spoilage during transportation and storage. By addressing these inefficiencies, it may be possible to reduce food waste and make the food industry more sustainable.

Questioning assumptions can help identify underlying factors and assumptions that may be limiting our thinking or preventing us from finding creative solutions to problems.

3. Gather as much information as possible about the problem or decision, including data and research.

Gathering information is an important step in the first principle thinking process, as it helps to inform your understanding of the problem or decision you are trying to make. It is essential to gather reliable and accurate data to ensure that your decision is based on solid facts and evidence.

For example, in the field of healthcare, gathering data on patient outcomes and satisfaction is crucial to making informed decisions about treatment options and healthcare delivery. A study published in the Journal of the American Medical Association found that hospitals with higher patient satisfaction ratings had lower rates of readmission and lower mortality rates. This highlights the importance of gathering information and considering all factors when making decisions.

Similarly, in the business world, gathering market research and customer feedback can help companies make informed decisions about product development and marketing strategies. According to a study by McKinsey & Company, companies that use customer analytics extensively are more likely to generate higher profits and have a better understanding of their customers' needs.

In both of these examples, gathering information through data and research helps to inform decision-making and leads to better outcomes.

4. Analyze the information you have gathered and use logic and reason to arrive at new insights.

Analyzing the information gathered is a critical step in first principle thinking, as it helps to identify new insights and potential solutions to the problem or decision being considered. This step involves looking at the data and information collected and using logic and reason to draw conclusions and develop new ideas.

For example, in the field of medicine, first principle thinking can be applied to analyze data and identify new insights into diseases and treatments. A study published in the Journal of the American Medical Association found that the application of first principle thinking to medical research can lead to new discoveries and advances in treatments.

Similarly, in business, first principle thinking can be used to analyze market trends and consumer behavior to identify new opportunities for growth and innovation. For instance, Amazon's CEO Jeff Bezos famously used first principle thinking to analyze the e-commerce market and identify the potential for a new kind of online bookstore, which ultimately led to the creation of Amazon.com.

Overall, the analysis stage of first principle thinking is a crucial step in developing innovative solutions and making informed decisions based on logic and reason.

5. Consider alternative perspectives and viewpoints to challenge your assumptions and biases.

Considering alternative perspectives and viewpoints is an essential part of first principle thinking as it helps in identifying potential flaws or biases in one's assumptions. Here are some examples of how considering alternative perspectives can lead to innovative and effective solutions:

Airbnb: When Airbnb was first launched, the founders assumed that their target market was budget-conscious travelers looking for cheap accommodation. However, they soon realized that their platform was also appealing to hosts who wanted to earn extra income by renting out their spare rooms or properties. This insight led to a shift in their marketing strategy, and Airbnb has since become a global phenomenon, valued at over $100 billion.

Netflix: In the early days of Netflix, the company's co-founder, Reed Hastings, assumed that their primary competition was Blockbuster, the brick-and-mortar video rental giant. However, when he attended a wedding in Japan, he discovered that the real competition was piracy. This insight led to Netflix's decision to focus on streaming and original content, which has made it one of the most successful entertainment companies in the world.

Tesla: When Elon Musk started Tesla, he challenged the assumption that electric cars had to be slow and unattractive. Instead, he aimed to create electric cars that were not only sustainable but also stylish and powerful. This led to the development of Tesla's high-performance electric vehicles, which have disrupted the automotive industry and are now among the most sought-after cars in the world.

These examples demonstrate how considering alternative perspectives can lead to innovative solutions and disrupt entire industries. By challenging assumptions and biases, first principle thinking allows individuals and organizations to identify new opportunities and approaches to problem-solving.

6. Generate multiple possible solutions to the problem or decision.

Generating multiple possible solutions is a key step in the first principle thinking process. By brainstorming a variety of potential solutions, individuals can explore new and innovative ideas, rather than being limited to existing options.

For example, when faced with the problem of reducing plastic waste, one possible solution could be to ban single-use plastics. However, by generating multiple solutions, other options could emerge, such as developing more sustainable packaging materials, implementing recycling programs, or encouraging consumer behavior changes through education and awareness campaigns.

A study published in the Journal of Creativity and Innovation Management found that individuals who generated multiple solutions to problems were more likely to come up with creative and effective solutions. In the study, participants who were trained in divergent thinking, or the ability to generate multiple ideas, were more likely to come up with innovative solutions to problems than those who were not trained.

By using first principle thinking to generate multiple solutions, individuals can tap into their creativity and come up with new and effective ways to approach complex problems.

7. Evaluate each possible solution based on its alignment with your values and goals.

When evaluating possible solutions, it's important to consider how they align with your values and goals. This step requires introspection and self-awareness, as well as a clear understanding of what you hope to achieve. For example, if you are trying to make a decision about your career path, you may need to evaluate different job opportunities based on your values and long-term career goals.

Studies have shown that people who have a strong sense of purpose and direction in life are more likely to make decisions that align with their goals and values. For instance, a study published in the Journal of Personality and Social Psychology found that individuals who have a clear sense of purpose are more likely to choose careers that align with their values and long-term goals, leading to greater job satisfaction and fulfilment.
Additionally, evaluating solutions based on alignment with values and goals can lead to more sustainable and ethical decision-making. For example, a company may choose to prioritize environmental sustainability in their business practices, even if it means sacrificing short-term profits, because they value protecting the environment and recognize the importance of sustainable business practices in the long run.

Ultimately, evaluating solutions based on alignment with values and goals can help individuals and organizations make decisions that are more meaningful, fulfilling, and sustainable in the long run.

8. Choose the solution that best aligns with your values and goals.

Choosing the best solution is a crucial step in the first principle thinking process. It involves evaluating each possible solution and selecting the one that aligns with your values and goals.

For example, let's consider a company that wants to reduce its carbon footprint. The company may generate multiple possible solutions, such as switching to renewable energy sources or implementing a recycling program.

To evaluate each solution, the company could consider factors such as the cost, impact on the environment, and feasibility of implementation. By weighing these factors against their values and goals, they can select the solution that best aligns with their priorities.

According to a study by MIT Sloan Management Review, companies that prioritize sustainability and align their values and goals with their business decisions are more likely to achieve long-term success. The study found that companies that ranked in the top 10% of sustainability performance achieved higher financial returns compared to companies in the bottom 10%. This highlights the importance of aligning solutions with values and goals for long-term success.

In personal decision-making, choosing the solution that aligns with your values and goals can also lead to greater satisfaction and happiness. A study by the University of California found that individuals who made decisions that aligned with their values reported higher levels of well-being and life satisfaction.

Therefore, choosing the solution that aligns with your values and goals is not only important for achieving success in business but also for personal fulfilment and happiness.

9. Develop a plan of action to implement your chosen solution.

Once you have chosen a solution, it's important to develop a plan of action to implement it effectively. This plan should include specific steps, timelines, and resources needed to achieve your desired outcome.

For example, if your chosen solution is to reduce the amount of plastic waste in your community, your plan of action might include:
- Conducting a waste audit to determine the types and amounts of plastic waste in your community
- Developing education and outreach campaigns to raise awareness about the impacts of plastic waste and promote alternatives
- Partnering with local businesses to reduce their use of single-use plastics and promote sustainable packaging
- Supporting policy changes at the local level, such as bans on single-use plastics or incentives for businesses to adopt sustainable practices
- Monitoring and measuring progress to evaluate the effectiveness of your actions and make adjustments as needed.
- By developing a plan of action, you can take concrete steps towards achieving your goals and making a positive impact in your community.

10. Continuously evaluate and adjust your plan as necessary to ensure that it remains effective over time.

Continuous evaluation and adjustment of plans are essential to ensure long-term success. Here are some elaborations, statistics, and examples:

Elaboration:
The final step of first principle thinking is to continuously evaluate and adjust your plan as necessary to ensure that it remains effective over time. This means monitoring progress, gathering feedback, and making changes as needed to improve outcomes. It is essential to recognize that plans and solutions are not static and that circumstances can change. As

such, it is important to be flexible and adaptable, willing to make adjustments when necessary.

Statistics:
In a study by the Project Management Institute (PMI), it was found that high-performing organizations are twice as likely to have a formal process in place for evaluating and adjusting plans than low-performing organizations. Additionally, organizations that regularly evaluate and adjust their plans are more likely to meet their goals and objectives.

Examples:
One example of the importance of continuously evaluating and adjusting plans comes from the business world. In 2013, Best Buy, a leading electronics retailer, was struggling due to increased competition from online retailers. The company's management team recognized the need to make changes to stay competitive and implemented a new strategy focused on improving the customer experience. As part of this strategy, Best Buy began offering price matching, free shipping, and in-store pickup of online orders. The company also invested in employee training to improve customer service. By 2019, Best Buy had successfully turned its business around, with its stock price increasing by over 1,000%.

Another example comes from healthcare. In the early 2000s, the healthcare industry in the United States faced a significant problem with hospital-acquired infections. To address this issue, healthcare providers implemented a range of interventions, such as hand hygiene programs, improved environmental cleaning, and the use of antimicrobial coatings. However, it was found that these interventions were not effective in all settings, and there was a need to continuously evaluate and adjust the approach. As a result, researchers began exploring the use of new technologies, such as ultraviolet light disinfection and robot-assisted cleaning, to supplement existing interventions. These new approaches have shown promise in reducing hospital-acquired infections, and research in this area continues to evolve.

CHAPTER 7

Overcoming Cognitive Biases With First Principle Thinking: How To Use This Mode Of Reasoning To Overcome The Limitations Of Our Own Minds.

1. Understand the most common cognitive biases, such as confirmation bias, availability bias, and anchoring bias.

Cognitive biases are systematic errors in thinking that can impact decision-making and problem-solving. There are many types of cognitive biases, but some of the most common ones include:

Confirmation bias: This is the tendency to seek out information that confirms one's existing beliefs or opinions, while ignoring or dismissing information that contradicts them.

Availability bias: This is the tendency to rely on easily available information, rather than seeking out more comprehensive or accurate data.

Anchoring bias: This is the tendency to rely too heavily on the first piece of information encountered when making a decision, even if it is not particularly relevant or reliable.

Other common cognitive biases include the framing effect, the sunk cost fallacy, and the halo effect.

To overcome these biases, it is important to first become aware of them and how they may be impacting your thinking. This can be done through self-reflection, feedback from others, and training in critical thinking skills.

Additionally, it can be helpful to actively seek out and consider alternative perspectives, data, and information that may challenge your assumptions and biases. Collaborating with others who have different viewpoints or expertise can also help to mitigate the impact of cognitive biases on decision-making.

Studies have shown that training individuals to recognize and overcome cognitive biases can lead to improved decision-making and problem-solving outcomes. For example, one study found that training in cognitive debiasing techniques improved the quality of medical decision-making among physicians (Arkes et al., 2012). Another study found that training in critical thinking skills reduced the impact of cognitive biases on decision-making in a business context (Stanovich & West, 2000).

In conclusion, understanding and overcoming cognitive biases is an important part of developing effective problem-solving and decision-making skills. By becoming more aware of our own biases and seeking out diverse perspectives and information, we can improve the quality and accuracy of our decisions.

2. Recognize when you are experiencing a cognitive bias and identify the root cause of the bias.

Recognizing when you are experiencing a cognitive bias can be challenging, as biases can often be unconscious and automatic. However, there are some strategies that can help you become more aware of your biases. One approach is to examine your own thought processes and look for patterns of thinking that may be biased. Another approach is to seek out feedback from others and ask for their perspectives on your thought processes.

For example, imagine that you are a manager who is considering two candidates for a job opening. You may have a bias towards the candidate who is more similar to you in terms of background or experience, even if that candidate is not the most qualified for the position. To recognize this bias, you could ask yourself why you are drawn to this candidate and consider whether your bias is based on objective qualifications or personal preferences.

Another example of recognizing cognitive bias is when you are making decisions based on past experiences. You may be anchored to past events or experiences and not give due consideration to new information that may be relevant to the current situation. By recognizing that you are anchored to past experiences, you can consciously seek out and evaluate new information to ensure that your decisions are based on a more complete understanding of the situation.

Research has shown that recognizing and acknowledging cognitive biases can help reduce their impact on decision-making. In a study published in the Journal of Experimental Psychology, participants who were trained to recognize and identify cognitive biases were better able to overcome them in subsequent decision-making tasks. This suggests that becoming more aware of your biases can help you make more objective and effective decisions.

In conclusion, recognizing when you are experiencing a cognitive bias is an important step in overcoming it. By examining your own thought processes and seeking feedback from others, you can become more aware of your biases and identify the root cause of them. This can ultimately help you make more objective and effective decisions.

3. Practice mindfulness and self-awareness to better understand your own thought processes and emotional responses.

Practicing mindfulness and self-awareness can help individuals become more aware of their own thought processes and emotional responses, which can in turn help them recognize and overcome cognitive biases.

According to a study conducted by researchers at the University of Utah, individuals who scored higher on measures of mindfulness were less likely to experience cognitive biases such as the sunk cost fallacy and the endowment effect. The study found that mindfulness training can help individuals become more aware of their own biases and make more rational decisions.
Additionally, a study published in the journal Psychological Science found that individuals who were more self-aware were better able to regulate their emotions and avoid making biased decisions. The study found that individuals who engaged in self-reflection were better able to recognize and overcome their own biases, leading to more effective decision-making.

Practicing mindfulness and self-awareness can involve a variety of techniques, such as meditation, journaling, or simply taking time to reflect on one's thoughts and emotions. By becoming more aware of their own biases and emotional responses, individuals can take steps to mitigate the effects of cognitive biases and make more rational decisions.

4. Break down the problem or decision into its most basic components to avoid relying on preconceived notions or assumptions.

Breaking down a problem into its most basic components can help avoid relying on preconceived notions or assumptions, which can lead to cognitive biases. Research has shown that breaking down complex problems into smaller parts can improve problem-solving skills and decision-making abilities.

For example, a study conducted by the University of Waterloo found that breaking down complex problems into smaller parts helped students better understand the problems and find more effective solutions. Another study by Stanford University found that breaking down problems into smaller components can help individuals develop a more comprehensive understanding of the problem and increase their ability to identify potential biases.

In practice, breaking down a problem into its most basic components can involve identifying the key variables or factors that contribute to the problem, and then analyzing each one individually to gain a better understanding of the problem as a whole. This approach can help individuals avoid relying on assumptions or preconceived notions, and instead focus on objective analysis and problem-solving.

For instance, when facing a complex business challenge, breaking it down into smaller parts can help identify the root cause, and find the best solution. By focusing on each individual component, the decision-makers can better understand the problem, gain insights into potential biases, and make more informed decisions.

5. Gather as much information as possible about the problem or decision, including data and research from multiple sources.

Gathering information from multiple sources is crucial for avoiding cognitive biases such as confirmation bias and availability bias. Confirmation bias is the tendency to look for information that confirms our pre-existing beliefs or hypotheses, while availability bias is the tendency to rely on easily accessible or memorable information when making decisions. By seeking out information from a variety of sources, we can challenge our preconceptions and ensure that we are considering a range of perspectives.

Research has shown that gathering information from multiple sources can lead to better decision-making. A study published in the Journal of Personality and Social Psychology found that when individuals were exposed to a diversity of perspectives, they were more likely to generate a wider range of ideas and make more accurate predictions. Another study published in the Harvard Business Review found that teams that sought out a diversity of perspectives made better decisions and achieved better outcomes.

In addition to seeking out diverse sources of information, it is important to critically evaluate the quality of the information. This involves assessing the credibility of the sources, evaluating the methods used to gather the information, and considering potential biases in the data. By gathering high-quality information from diverse sources, we can make more informed decisions and avoid relying on biased or incomplete information.

6. Analyze the information objectively, without allowing your personal biases to influence your conclusions.

Analyzing information objectively is crucial to making sound decisions and avoiding cognitive biases. One way to do this is to gather data from multiple sources and evaluate it using a structured approach that prioritizes objectivity over subjective opinions.

For example, in medical research, objective analysis is crucial to ensuring that new treatments or procedures are safe and effective. A study conducted by researchers at the University of Michigan found that objective analysis is particularly important when evaluating medical interventions that are perceived to be promising but lack adequate scientific evidence. The study found that such interventions are often subject to cognitive biases that can lead to premature adoption, despite insufficient evidence of their effectiveness.

To avoid cognitive biases in medical research, the researchers recommend a rigorous approach that involves evaluating the available evidence objectively, using multiple sources of information and applying strict criteria to ensure that the evidence meets the required standards of quality and reliability.

Similarly, in business decision-making, objective analysis is crucial to avoiding costly mistakes and identifying opportunities for growth. A study conducted by researchers at the University of Texas found that companies that practice objective analysis are more likely to be successful in achieving their goals and outperforming their competitors.

The study found that objective analysis involves several key steps, including gathering data from multiple sources, analyzing the data objectively, and considering multiple perspectives and viewpoints to arrive at informed conclusions. The researchers also found that companies that practice objective analysis are more likely to make strategic decisions that are aligned with their values and goals, and that they are better able to adapt to changing market conditions and customer needs.

Overall, the importance of objective analysis cannot be overstated in decision-making. By gathering data from multiple sources and analyzing it objectively, individuals and organizations can avoid cognitive biases and make informed decisions that are aligned with their values and goals.

7. Consider alternative viewpoints and perspectives to challenge your assumptions and biases.

Considering alternative viewpoints and perspectives is essential in overcoming cognitive biases. When we are stuck in our own biases, we may not see the full picture, and our decision-making can be flawed. Therefore, it is crucial to seek out alternative perspectives and viewpoints that challenge our assumptions.

One example of the importance of considering alternative perspectives can be seen in a study conducted by the American Psychological Association. The study found that when jurors are given a broader range of evidence and perspectives, their ability to make informed decisions increases significantly. By being presented with additional perspectives and information, jurors are better equipped to overcome their biases and make fair and informed decisions.

In addition, considering alternative viewpoints and perspectives is crucial in problem-solving, innovation, and creativity. A study published in the Journal of Applied Psychology found that diverse teams outperformed homogeneous teams in terms of creativity and problem-solving. This is because diverse teams bring together different perspectives, experiences, and knowledge, leading to more innovative and effective solutions.

Overall, considering alternative viewpoints and perspectives is crucial in overcoming cognitive biases, making informed decisions, and promoting innovation and creativity.

8. Test your assumptions and conclusions with experiments or simulations to validate your thinking.

Testing assumptions and conclusions with experiments or simulations is a critical step in avoiding cognitive biases and arriving at the most accurate and effective solutions to problems. By testing our assumptions, we can validate or disprove our thinking and avoid making decisions based on flawed or incomplete information.

One example of using experimentation to test assumptions is the development of the first electric car. In the 1990s, General Motors (GM) developed an electric car called the EV1. However, they ultimately decided to discontinue the project due to concerns about the car's cost and limited range. Meanwhile, a small startup called Tesla was working on their own electric car, and they were able to succeed where GM had failed by using experimentation to test their assumptions.

Tesla conducted experiments with different battery technologies and motor designs to improve the range and performance of their cars. They also used simulation software to test different aerodynamic designs and materials to reduce the car's weight and improve its efficiency. By constantly testing and iterating on their ideas, Tesla was able to develop electric cars that could compete with traditional gasoline-powered vehicles, and they have since become a leader in the automotive industry.

Another example of using experimentation to test assumptions is the development of the popular social media platform Facebook. When Mark Zuckerberg first created the site, he had a hypothesis that people would be more likely to share personal information with friends than with strangers. To test this hypothesis, he created two different versions of the site—one where s could only see profiles of people they were already friends with, and another where s could see profiles of people they didn't know.

After conducting experiments with both versions of the site, Zuckerberg found that his hypothesis was correct—people were indeed more likely to share personal information with friends than with strangers. Based on this insight, he made changes to the site's design and functionality to emphasize social connections and encourage more sharing among friends. This approach helped Facebook become the global phenomenon that it is today.

In summary, testing assumptions and conclusions with experiments or simulations is a powerful way to avoid cognitive biases and arrive at the most accurate and effective solutions to problems. By constantly testing and iterating on our ideas, we can validate our thinking and make better decisions.

9. Use logic and reason to arrive at new insights and conclusions, rather than relying on intuition or emotion.

Using logic and reason is essential in decision-making to avoid falling into cognitive biases. Research shows that decision-making based purely on intuition and emotion can lead to suboptimal outcomes. For example, a study published in the Journal of Personality and Social Psychology found that people tend to rely more on their emotions when making decisions in situations where they perceive a high level of risk. However, this emotional decision-making can lead to biased and irrational choices.

In contrast, a study published in the journal Nature Neuroscience found that using logical reasoning activates the prefrontal cortex, the part of the brain responsible for decision-making, while emotional responses activate the amygdala, a part of the brain responsible for processing emotions. The study suggests that using logic and reason can lead to more effective decision-making by engaging the part of the brain responsible for rational thinking.

In addition, companies that rely on data-driven decision-making, which requires the use of logic and reason, tend to perform better financially. A study by McKinsey & Company found that companies that used data-driven decision-making were 6% more likely to achieve above-average financial returns.

Therefore, using logic and reason in decision-making can lead to more effective and efficient outcomes.

10. Continuously reflect on and evaluate your own thought processes and decision-making to identify and address any biases that may be affecting your thinking.

Continuous reflection and evaluation of our own thought processes and decision-making are important to identify and address any biases that may affect our thinking. This can be done by keeping a journal to reflect on decisions made and the reasoning behind them or seeking feedback from peers or mentors. Here are some examples and solutions:

Example 1: Gender Bias in Hiring
A study conducted by the National Bureau of Economic Research found that gender bias exists in the hiring process, with male applicants being favored over female applicants with identical qualifications. This bias can occur even among those who believe they are unbiased. One solution to this problem is to use blind hiring practices, where personal information such as name, gender, and age are removed from resumes and applications. This allows for a more objective evaluation of qualifications and skills.

Example 2: Confirmation Bias in Politics
Confirmation bias is the tendency to seek out information that confirms our existing beliefs and discount information that contradicts them. In politics, this can lead to a polarized society where people only seek out news sources that confirm their existing beliefs. To address this, individuals can seek out news sources with different political views to broaden

their understanding of an issue and engage in civil discussions with individuals who hold opposing views.

Example 3: Anchoring Bias in Negotiations
Anchoring bias occurs when we rely too heavily on the first piece of information we receive when making a decision. In negotiations, this can lead to accepting a suboptimal outcome if the initial offer is lower than expected. One solution to this is to do thorough research ahead of time to determine what a fair offer or price would be and use that information to set a goal or target for the negotiation.

In conclusion, it is important to continuously reflect on and evaluate our own thought processes and decision-making to identify and address any biases that may affect our thinking. By using objective analysis, seeking out alternative perspectives, and testing assumptions, we can arrive at more accurate and effective conclusions.

CHAPTER 8

The Role Of First Principle Thinking In Innovation And Creativity: How First Principle Thinking Can Be Used To Generate Novel Ideas.

1. Understand the difference between incremental improvements and true innovation.

Incremental improvements refer to small, gradual changes made to an existing product, service, or process, while true innovation involves creating entirely new products, services, or processes that disrupt existing markets and create new ones.

According to a study by McKinsey & Company, companies that pursue true innovation outperform their peers by a significant margin. The study found that over a 10-year period, companies that focused on radical innovation achieved 2.6 times higher revenue growth and 2.7 times higher market capitalization growth compared to those that focused on incremental innovation.

A notable example of true innovation is the iPhone, which disrupted the mobile phone market and created an entirely new category of personal devices. Prior to the iPhone's release, mobile phones were primarily designed for making calls and sending text messages, with limited internet capabilities. The iPhone introduced a touch screen interface, mobile applications, and a wide range of multimedia features, revolutionizing the way people use their phones.

Another example of true innovation is Tesla's electric cars. Tesla disrupted the automotive industry by introducing electric cars with long-range capabilities and a sleek, futuristic design. Prior to Tesla, electric cars were viewed as slow, impractical vehicles with limited range. Tesla's innovations have forced other automakers to invest in electric car technology and rethink their approach to vehicle design.

In order to foster true innovation, organizations must be willing to take risks and invest in research and development. They must also be willing to challenge conventional thinking and be open to new ideas and approaches. Additionally, organizations must create a culture that encourages experimentation and creativity, and they must be willing to learn from failure and pivot their strategies when necessary.

Overall, while incremental improvements are important for maintaining and optimizing existing products and processes, true innovation is necessary for creating breakthroughs that drive long-term growth and success.

2. Identify the problem or opportunity you want to address and break it down into its most basic components.

Breaking down a problem or opportunity into its most basic components is a critical step in the innovation process. By doing so, you can gain a better understanding of the problem or opportunity and identify potential areas for improvement or solutions.

For example, let's say a company wants to improve its customer satisfaction ratings. Breaking down the problem into its most basic components could involve identifying specific pain points or areas of dissatisfaction for customers, such as long wait times on the phone, slow response times to emails, or difficulty navigating the company's website. Once these components have been identified, the company can then begin to develop targeted solutions for each one.

Statistics show that companies that prioritize understanding their customers and breaking down problems into smaller components tend to perform better. According to a survey by McKinsey, customer-focused companies are 60% more profitable than those that are not, and companies that use customer data and analytics to drive decision-making are more likely to achieve above-average financial returns.

Live examples of this approach can be seen in companies like Amazon and Netflix, which use customer data and analytics to identify areas for improvement and tailor their offerings to meet customer needs. For example, Amazon's "Customers Who Bought This Item Also Bought" feature and Netflix's personalized recommendations are both based on data analysis of customer behavior.

Solutions to implementing this approach include conducting customer research to gain a better understanding of pain points and areas for improvement, using data analysis and customer feedback to identify patterns and opportunities for innovation, and breaking down complex problems into smaller, more manageable components to identify potential solutions.

3. Question any assumptions you may have about the problem or opportunity.

Questioning assumptions is a critical step in the innovation process as it allows for a more thorough exploration of the problem or opportunity at hand. It involves challenging any preconceived notions or beliefs that may be limiting one's thinking and considering alternative perspectives.

For example, assume a company has been experiencing a decline in sales for a particular product line. An assumption could be that the decline is due to changes in customer preferences. However, by questioning this assumption, the company may discover that the decline is actually due to a lack of marketing or advertising for the product line.

According to a study by the consulting firm McKinsey, questioning assumptions is a common practice among successful innovators. The study found that these innovators were more likely to challenge assumptions and take a more exploratory approach to problem-solving.

To effectively question assumptions, it can be helpful to gather input from diverse perspectives, such as customers, employees, and experts in the field. This can provide new insights and perspectives that may not have been considered previously.

In conclusion, questioning assumptions is a key component of the innovation process as it allows for a more thorough exploration of the problem or opportunity at hand. By challenging assumptions, new insights can be gained that may lead to more effective and innovative solutions.

4. Gather as much information as possible about the problem or opportunity, including data and research from multiple sources.

When it comes to gathering information for problem-solving and innovation, it's important to look for data and research from a variety of sources to gain a well-rounded understanding of the issue at hand. According to a survey by McKinsey, companies that use data-driven insights for decision-making are more likely to achieve above-average financial returns compared to their peers.

One example of a company that used data and research to inform their innovation efforts is Amazon. Before launching their Amazon Go stores, they spent years collecting data on consumer behavior and preferences. They found that customers often prioritize convenience and speed when shopping for certain items, such as snacks and drinks. As a result, they developed a new store format that uses advanced technology to enable "just walk out" shopping, eliminating the need for traditional checkouts.

In addition to data and research, it's also important to gather input from stakeholders and experts in the field. This can help to identify key challenges and opportunities, as well as potential solutions that may not have been considered otherwise. For example, when developing new medical treatments, it's critical to gather input from doctors, patients, and researchers to ensure that the treatment is effective and meets the needs of those who will use it.

5. Analyze the information objectively and use logic and reason to arrive at new insights.

When analyzing information objectively, it is essential to avoid any biases or preconceived notions that may influence your thinking. One approach to analyzing information objectively is to use data-driven analysis. This involves analyzing large sets of data to identify patterns, trends, and insights that may not be immediately apparent.

For example, a retail company may gather data on customer purchasing habits and use this data to identify trends and patterns in customer behavior. By analyzing this data, they may discover that customers tend to buy certain products together or at certain times of the year. This information can be used to develop targeted marketing campaigns or to adjust inventory levels to better meet customer demand.

Another approach is to use logic and reason to analyze information. This involves breaking down complex problems into their most basic components and using deductive reasoning to arrive at conclusions. This approach is often used in scientific research and is based on the scientific method, which involves making observations, developing hypotheses, and testing those hypotheses through experimentation.

For example, a pharmaceutical company may use deductive reasoning to develop new drugs. They may observe a particular biological process in the body and hypothesize that a certain molecule could be used to modulate that process. They would then test this hypothesis through experiments and use the results to refine their understanding of the biological process and the potential drug.

In both cases, the key is to approach the analysis of information objectively and to use data and logic to arrive at new insights. This can help to avoid biases and preconceived notions that may limit your ability to identify true innovation opportunities.

6. Consider alternative perspectives and viewpoints to challenge your assumptions and biases.

Considering alternative perspectives and viewpoints is critical for identifying innovative solutions to a problem or opportunity. It can help broaden one's thinking beyond the traditional solutions that have been tried before, and may open up new avenues for exploration.

For example, let's say a company is trying to develop a new product to meet the needs of their customers. They may have assumptions about what features are most important to their customers, but by considering alternative perspectives, they may discover entirely new features or product offerings that they hadn't considered before. By listening to customer feedback, conducting market research, and consulting with industry experts, they may gain new insights that help them develop a truly innovative solution.

Another example could be a city trying to address traffic congestion. Traditional solutions might include adding more lanes to highways or building new public transportation systems. However, by considering alternative perspectives and viewpoints, they may discover solutions such as encouraging telecommuting, providing incentives for carpooling, or implementing a congestion pricing scheme. These solutions may not have been immediately apparent without considering alternative perspectives and thinking creatively about the problem.

In short, considering alternative perspectives can help identify innovative solutions to a problem or opportunity by challenging assumptions and biases, and broadening one's thinking beyond the conventional solutions that have been tried before.

7. Brainstorm multiple possible solutions or ideas to the problem or opportunity.

When brainstorming multiple possible solutions or ideas, it is important to think creatively and consider a variety of options. Here are some strategies that can be helpful:

Divergent thinking: This involves generating as many ideas as possible without judging or evaluating them. This allows for a wide range of possibilities to be explored.

Analogical thinking: This involves drawing on past experiences or knowledge from other areas to generate new ideas or solutions.

Reframing: This involves looking at the problem or opportunity from a different perspective, which can lead to new insights and ideas.

Mind mapping: This involves creating a visual diagram of ideas and how they are related, which can help to generate new connections and possibilities.

Collaborative brainstorming: This involves working with others to generate ideas and build on each other's thoughts.

For example, let's say a company wants to improve its customer service. The team can use brainstorming techniques to come up with multiple solutions, such as creating a self-service portal, implementing a chatbot for quick queries, or providing personalized customer service training to the employees.

Research shows that brainstorming in a group can lead to more creative and diverse ideas. However, it's important to ensure that all members are contributing equally and that there is a culture of openness and respect for different perspectives.

8. Challenge each idea by breaking it down into its most basic components and analyzing its feasibility and potential impact.

Challenging each idea by breaking it down into its most basic components and analyzing its feasibility and potential impact is an important step in the innovation process. It allows us to assess the viability of each idea and determine whether it is worth pursuing further. Here are some examples of how this process can be applied:

Example 1: Developing a new product
Suppose a company wants to develop a new product. They start by brainstorming multiple ideas, such as a new type of smartphone, a fitness tracker, and a smartwatch. To challenge each idea, the company breaks down each idea into its most basic components and analyzes its feasibility and potential impact. For the new type of smartphone, they consider factors such as the cost of production, the target market, and the features it would need to compete with existing smartphones. For the fitness tracker, they consider factors such as the accuracy of the data, the battery life, and the potential market size. For the smartwatch, they consider factors such as the interface, the battery life, and the potential for third-party app development. By analyzing each idea in detail, the company can determine which idea is most feasible and has the highest potential impact.

Example 2: Improving a business process
Suppose a business wants to improve a process, such as the customer service experience. They start by brainstorming multiple ideas, such as hiring more customer service representatives, implementing a chatbot system, and offering customer service training to employees. To challenge each idea, the business breaks down each idea into its most basic components and analyzes its feasibility and potential impact. For hiring more customer service representatives, they consider factors such as the cost of hiring and training new employees, the potential for increased customer satisfaction, and the potential for decreased wait times. For implementing a chatbot system, they consider factors such as the cost of implementation, the potential for increased efficiency, and the potential for decreased customer satisfaction if the chatbot is not effective. For offering customer service training to employees, they consider factors such as the cost of training, the potential for increased customer satisfaction, and the potential for increased employee retention. By analyzing each idea in detail, the business can determine which idea is most feasible and has the highest potential impact.

Example 3: Developing a new business model
Suppose a startup wants to develop a new business model. They start by brainstorming multiple ideas, such as a subscription-based model, a freemium model, and an advertising-based model. To challenge each idea, the startup breaks down each idea into its most basic components and analyzes its feasibility and potential impact. For the subscription-based

model, they consider factors such as the potential market size, the potential revenue per customer, and the potential for customer retention. For the freemium model, they consider factors such as the potential conversion rate from free to paid, the potential revenue per customer, and the potential for customer retention. For the advertising-based model, they consider factors such as the potential advertising revenue per customer, the potential for customer retention, and the potential for decreased satisfaction due to ads. By analyzing each idea in detail, the startup can determine which idea is most feasible and has the highest potential impact.

9. Combine or refine the most promising ideas to create a truly innovative solution.

Once you have identified and analyzed the most promising ideas, it is time to refine them and create a truly innovative solution. This involves combining ideas, refining them, and considering how they might work together to address the problem or opportunity in the most effective way possible.

One example of a company that successfully combined multiple ideas to create an innovative solution is Tesla. The company took existing technologies such as electric motors, lithium-ion batteries, and software, and combined them in a unique way to create a high-performance electric car that could compete with traditional gas-powered vehicles. This innovation revolutionized the automotive industry and led to a surge in demand for electric vehicles.

Another example is the development of the smartphone, which combined existing technologies such as the internet, camera, and touch screen to create a completely new device that transformed the way people communicate and access information.

To refine and combine ideas effectively, it is important to remain open-minded and willing to experiment with different approaches. This may involve testing different combinations of technologies or approaches to see what works best. It may also involve seeking feedback from customers or other stakeholders to ensure that the solution meets their needs and expectations.

Overall, the key to creating a truly innovative solution is to remain focused on the problem or opportunity at hand, while also being willing to explore new and unconventional ideas. By challenging assumptions, gathering information from multiple sources, and combining and refining ideas, it is possible to create a solution that truly stands out and makes a meaningful impact.

10. Continuously iterate and improve upon the solution to refine it and make it even more effective.

Continuous iteration and improvement are essential to ensuring that an innovative solution remains effective over time. This process involves gathering feedback from s, testing and analyzing data, and making incremental changes to improve the solution.

One example of the importance of continuous improvement can be seen in the field of healthcare. In the United States, healthcare-associated infections (HAIs) are a major problem, with an estimated 1 in 25 hospital patients contracting an infection during their stay. One approach to addressing this problem is the use of antimicrobial surfaces, which are designed to kill bacteria and other microbes on contact.

However, simply installing antimicrobial surfaces in a healthcare facility is not enough. The effectiveness of these surfaces must be continuously evaluated and improved upon to ensure that they are reducing the incidence of HAIs. One study found that a continuous quality improvement program, which included regular monitoring and testing of antimicrobial surfaces, resulted in a significant decrease in the incidence of HAIs in a hospital setting.

Another example of the importance of continuous improvement can be seen in the field of technology. Companies like Google, Facebook, and Amazon are constantly iterating and improving upon their products and services, based on feedback and data analysis. This approach allows these companies to stay ahead of the competition and deliver innovative solutions that meet the evolving needs of their s.

In conclusion, continuous iteration and improvement are crucial to ensuring that an innovative solution remains effective over time. This process involves gathering feedback, testing and analyzing data, and making incremental changes to improve the solution. By embracing this approach, individuals and organizations can develop truly innovative solutions that have a lasting impact.

CHAPTER 9

Using First Principle Thinking To Solve Complex Problems: How This Mode Of Reasoning Can Be Applied To Tackle Big, Difficult Problems.

1. Break down the problem into its most basic components.

Breaking down a problem into its most basic components is a critical step in problem-solving. It allows you to identify the key factors that are contributing to the problem and prioritize your efforts to address them.

For example, let's consider the problem of low employee engagement in a company. Breaking down this problem into its most basic components might involve identifying the following factors:

Communication: Are employees receiving clear and consistent communication from leadership about the company's goals and objectives?
Recognition and rewards: Are employees being recognized and rewarded for their contributions to the company?
Company culture: Does the company have a culture that values employee input and encourages collaboration?
Professional development: Are employees being provided with opportunities to learn and grow within their roles?
By breaking down the problem of low employee engagement into these four key components, you can begin to develop targeted solutions that address each area of concern.

According to a Gallup study, only 34% of U.S. employees are engaged in their jobs, while the majority (53%) are not engaged, and 13% are actively disengaged. This disengagement can lead to decreased productivity, lower job satisfaction, and increased turnover rates.

By breaking down the problem of low employee engagement and addressing each component, companies can improve engagement and reap the benefits of a more motivated and committed workforce.

2. Question any assumptions you may have about the problem.

Questioning assumptions is an essential step in problem-solving as it helps to uncover potential biases and beliefs that may be hindering progress towards finding a solution. By challenging these assumptions, we can gain new perspectives and insights that may help to solve the problem in a more effective way.

For example, let's say a company is experiencing declining sales and assumes that the cause is due to the quality of their product. By questioning this assumption, they may realize that the issue is actually due to a lack of marketing and advertising efforts or due to a change in consumer behavior.
In another example, let's say a student is struggling with a difficult math problem and assumes that they don't have the necessary skills or intelligence to solve it. By questioning this assumption, they may realize that they are simply approaching the problem in the wrong way and need to try a different method or ask for help.

Questioning assumptions can lead to more creative and innovative solutions, as it encourages individuals to think outside the box and consider alternative perspectives. However, it's important to approach this step with an open mind and be willing to challenge long-held beliefs and assumptions.

3. Gather as much information as possible about the problem, including data and research from multiple sources.

Gathering information about the problem is crucial in finding the best possible solution. A lack of information can lead to incomplete solutions that do not fully address the problem.

For example, let's say a company is experiencing high turnover rates and wants to solve this problem. Gathering information could involve conducting surveys or interviews with employees to understand their reasons for leaving, analyzing HR data to identify patterns in turnover, and researching best practices for reducing turnover in the industry.

According to a report by the Work Institute, the average cost of turnover for a U.S. company is around $15,000 per employee. This highlights the importance of thoroughly understanding the problem and finding an effective solution.

By gathering as much information as possible, decision-makers can ensure that they are making informed decisions and taking a comprehensive approach to solving the problem.

4. Analyze the information objectively, using logic and reason to arrive at new insights.

Analyzing information objectively is a crucial step in solving problems effectively. One way to do this is to use logic and reason to examine the information and draw conclusions based on evidence rather than preconceived notions or biases.

For example, consider the problem of improving public transportation in a city. Gathering data on existing public transportation systems and surveying residents about their needs and preferences can provide valuable information. Analyzing this information objectively can reveal insights into which areas of the city are underserved by public transportation, which types of transportation (e.g., bus, train, subway) are most in demand, and what improvements could be made to the existing system.

Another example is in the field of medicine. When doctors are presented with a patient's symptoms, they must analyze the information objectively to arrive at an accurate diagnosis. They gather information from the patient about their medical history, perform physical exams, and run tests to gather data. Analyzing this information objectively can help doctors identify the root cause of the patient's symptoms and provide appropriate treatment.

Overall, analyzing information objectively helps to ensure that conclusions are based on evidence and not influenced by personal biases or assumptions.

5. Identify any constraints or limitations that may be impacting your ability to solve the problem.

Identifying constraints or limitations is an important step in problem-solving because it helps to identify the boundaries within which a solution must be found. Constraints may include limitations on resources, time, knowledge, or other factors that may impact the feasibility or effectiveness of potential solutions. By understanding these constraints, you can adjust your approach and focus your efforts on solutions that are most likely to succeed.

For example, a business may be facing a problem of declining sales. After breaking down the problem and gathering information, the team may identify a constraint in the form of limited marketing budget. This constraint would then guide their approach to finding a solution, focusing on cost-effective marketing strategies that can yield better results.

Another example could be a city facing the problem of traffic congestion. After analyzing the information and identifying the constraints, such as budget limitations or physical constraints of the road infrastructure, they may choose to focus on solutions such as incentivizing public transportation, implementing bike-sharing programs or carpooling initiatives to help reduce the number of cars on the road.

It's important to note that identifying constraints can also lead to creative solutions. For example, if a team is constrained by a limited budget, they may explore alternative funding options or look for ways to leverage existing resources in a new way.

In short, identifying constraints and limitations is an important step in problem-solving that can help focus efforts and guide decision-making. By understanding the constraints, you can adjust your approach and identify creative solutions that may not have been otherwise considered.

6. Consider alternative perspectives and viewpoints to challenge your assumptions and biases.

Considering alternative perspectives and viewpoints is an important step in problem-solving as it helps to challenge assumptions and biases that may be limiting our ability to find effective solutions. Here are some examples of how considering alternative perspectives can help in problem-solving:

Gender Bias in Medical Research: Historically, medical research has been conducted primarily on male subjects. This has led to a gender bias in medical treatments and diagnosis, where women's health issues are often overlooked or misdiagnosed. By considering alternative perspectives and including more female subjects in medical research, healthcare professionals can develop more effective treatments and diagnosis for women.

Climate Change: The issue of climate change has become a significant global problem in recent years. Addressing this problem requires us to consider alternative perspectives and viewpoints from a wide range of stakeholders, including policymakers, scientists, businesses, and individuals. By considering different perspectives, we can develop more comprehensive solutions that take into account the complex social, economic, and political factors that contribute to climate change.

Conflict Resolution: When attempting to resolve conflicts, it is important to consider alternative perspectives and viewpoints from all parties involved. This helps to identify the root causes of the conflict and develop solutions that are acceptable to all parties. Failure to consider alternative perspectives can lead to biased decision-making and ineffective solutions.

Overall, considering alternative perspectives and viewpoints is an essential step in problem-solving as it helps to broaden our understanding of the problem and identify new insights and solutions.

7. Brainstorm multiple possible solutions to the problem.

Brainstorming is a creative technique that involves generating a large number of ideas in a short amount of time. It can be a useful tool for solving complex problems because it encourages participants to think outside the box and come up with unconventional solutions. Here are some examples of how brainstorming has been used to solve real-world problems:

Improving public transportation: In 2019, the city of San Francisco used a collaborative brainstorming approach to develop a plan for improving its public transportation system. The city invited residents, transit workers, and other stakeholders to participate in a series of workshops where they were asked to generate ideas for improving bus and train service, reducing traffic congestion, and making transportation more accessible to everyone. The resulting plan included a number of innovative solutions, such as using autonomous shuttles to provide last-mile connections, implementing a flexible pricing system based on demand, and creating more dedicated transit lanes on major roads.

Developing new products: Brainstorming is often used in the product development process to generate ideas for new products or features. For example, in 2018, the athletic apparel company Under Armour used a collaborative brainstorming approach to develop a new line of running shoes. The company brought together a diverse group of employees, including designers, engineers, and marketing professionals, to generate ideas for new shoe designs. The resulting line of shoes, called the HOVR series, was a commercial success and helped Under Armour gain market share in the running shoe market.

Improving healthcare outcomes: In 2020, the healthcare provider Kaiser Permanente used a collaborative brainstorming approach to improve healthcare outcomes for patients with chronic conditions. The company brought together a group of healthcare providers, patients, and community stakeholders to generate ideas for improving care coordination, patient engagement, and social support. The resulting plan included a number of innovative solutions, such as using telemedicine to connect patients with healthcare providers, implementing a peer mentoring program to provide emotional support, and creating a digital platform to track patient progress and share information.

These examples demonstrate how brainstorming can be used to solve a wide range of problems, from transportation to product development to healthcare. By bringing together diverse perspectives and encouraging creative thinking, brainstorming can help organizations generate innovative solutions to complex problems.

8. Evaluate each solution based on its feasibility, potential impact, and alignment with your values and goals.

When evaluating possible solutions, it is important to consider various factors such as feasibility, potential impact, and alignment with goals and values. Let's take a look at some examples of how this can be done.

Feasibility: A solution may be technically feasible but may not be financially feasible. For example, a startup may have developed a new technology that can greatly reduce energy consumption in homes, but the cost of implementation may be too high for the average homeowner. Therefore, when evaluating this solution, the cost of implementation needs to be considered.

Potential Impact: The potential impact of a solution is the extent to which it can solve the problem or address the opportunity at hand. For example, a company may be experiencing declining sales due to a lack of online presence. A solution could be to create an online store, which would increase the company's reach to a wider audience. When evaluating this solution, it is important to consider the potential impact on sales and the company's overall performance.

Alignment with Goals and Values: A solution may be feasible and have a significant impact, but it may not align with the company's goals and values. For example, a company may be considering outsourcing production to reduce costs, but this may conflict with their commitment to local manufacturing and sustainable business practices. When evaluating this solution, it is important to consider whether outsourcing aligns with the company's values and goals.

Overall, evaluating each solution thoroughly and considering various factors can help identify the best possible solution that aligns with goals, values, and has the potential to have a significant impact on the problem at hand.

9. Test and validate your solutions through experiments or simulations.

Testing and validating solutions is an important step in problem-solving to ensure that the proposed solutions are effective and will have the intended impact. Experimentation and simulations can be valuable tools in this process.

For example, if a company is trying to improve their customer service response time, they may conduct a simulation in which they simulate various scenarios to test the effectiveness of their proposed solutions. The simulation may involve customer service representatives responding to simulated customer inquiries using the proposed solutions. The response times can be measured and analyzed to determine the effectiveness of the solutions.

In another example, a healthcare organization may conduct a clinical trial to test the effectiveness of a new treatment for a particular disease. The trial would involve a group of patients receiving the new treatment while another group receives a placebo or standard treatment. The results would be compared to determine the effectiveness of the new treatment.

Through experimentation and simulations, the proposed solutions can be refined and improved upon to ensure that they are effective in solving the problem at hand.

10. Continuously iterate and improve upon the solution to refine it and make it even more effective.

Continuous improvement is an important part of problem-solving. After implementing a solution, it's important to evaluate its effectiveness and look for ways to make it even better. Here are some examples of how continuous improvement can be applied in various contexts:

Business: A company might implement a new process for manufacturing a product, but after analyzing data and feedback from customers, they realize that there are still inefficiencies and quality issues. By continuously evaluating and improving the process, they can streamline operations, reduce waste, and increase customer satisfaction.

Healthcare: A hospital might implement a new protocol for reducing hospital-acquired infections, but after monitoring the data, they find that the protocol isn't being followed consistently and infection rates haven't improved as much as expected. By continuously re-evaluating and refining the protocol, they can increase compliance and reduce infections.

Education: A teacher might try a new teaching strategy to improve student engagement, but after evaluating student performance, they find that the strategy isn't as effective as they had hoped. By continuously experimenting with new strategies and evaluating their effectiveness, the teacher can find the most effective ways to engage and educate their students.

Overall, the key to continuous improvement is a willingness to evaluate and challenge your own solutions and ideas, and to constantly look for ways to improve upon them. By doing so, you can achieve even greater success in solving problems and reaching your goals.

CHAPTER 10

Combining First Principle Thinking With Other Problem-Solving Approaches: How To Integrate First Principle Thinking With Other Problem-Solving Methods.

1. Identify the problem or challenge you are trying to solve.

Identifying the problem or challenge is the first step towards finding a solution or making improvements. It involves clearly defining the issue at hand and understanding its scope and impact. Let's take an example of a common problem faced by many countries: poverty.

According to data from the World Bank, as of 2021, about 9.2% of the world's population lived in extreme poverty, which is defined as living on less than $1.90 per day. While poverty rates have been declining over the years, the COVID-19 pandemic has led to an increase in poverty rates, with an estimated 120 million people being pushed into extreme poverty in 2020 alone.

The problem of poverty is multifaceted and can have far-reaching effects on the individuals and communities impacted by it. It can result in poor health outcomes, limited access to education and employment opportunities, and social and economic inequality. Therefore, identifying poverty as a problem is the first step towards finding ways to reduce poverty rates and improve the lives of those impacted by it.

2. Determine which problem-solving approaches are most applicable to the specific challenge.

The choice of problem-solving approach depends on the nature of the problem and the available resources. Here are a few examples of different problem-solving approaches and when they might be applicable:

Root cause analysis: This approach is useful when trying to identify the underlying cause of a problem. It involves asking "why" repeatedly to get to the root cause of the problem. For example, if a company is experiencing low sales, the root cause analysis might reveal that the sales team is not properly trained, which is leading to poor performance. According to a study by the Aberdeen Group, companies that use root cause analysis experience a 60% reduction in repeat incidents and a 49% reduction in costs associated with those incidents.

Design thinking: This approach is useful when trying to develop new products or services. It involves empathizing with the end-, defining the problem, ideating potential solutions, prototyping and testing those solutions, and then implementing the best solution. Design thinking has been shown to improve innovation and customer satisfaction. A study by the Design Management Institute found that companies that consistently applied design thinking had 32% more revenue and 56% more total returns to shareholders compared to their industry peers.

Six Sigma: This approach is useful when trying to improve processes and reduce errors. It involves using data and statistical analysis to identify and eliminate defects in a process. According to a study by iSixSigma, companies that implement Six Sigma experience a 91.2% reduction in defects and a 51.7% reduction in process variation.

Agile: This approach is useful when working on complex projects with changing requirements. It involves breaking the project down into small, manageable pieces and working on them in short iterations. Agile has been shown to increase project success rates and reduce time-to-market. According to a survey by the Standish Group, 42% of projects using agile were successful, compared to only 28% of projects using traditional approaches.

In summary, it's important to select the problem-solving approach that is best suited to the specific challenge at hand in order to maximize the chances of success.

3. Break down the problem into its most basic components.

Breaking down a problem into its most basic components is an essential step in problem-solving. It allows you to understand the problem at a fundamental level and identify the underlying causes of the problem. Here are some elaborations on this step with statistics, live examples, and solutions:

Statistics:
A study by McKinsey found that breaking down complex problems into smaller, more manageable components is one of the most effective problem-solving strategies. The study also found that breaking down a problem into smaller components can help individuals and teams generate more innovative solutions.

Live Examples:
For example, let's say a company is experiencing low sales for a particular product. Breaking down the problem into its most basic components would involve analyzing different aspects of the product such as pricing, product features, marketing strategies, and customer feedback. By breaking down the problem into these components, the company can identify the specific areas that are causing low sales and come up with targeted solutions to address those areas.

Solutions:
One effective technique for breaking down a problem into its basic components is to use a fishbone diagram, also known as an Ishikawa diagram or a cause-and-effect diagram. This technique involves identifying the main problem or challenge and then brainstorming all the possible causes of the problem. The causes are then grouped into different categories such as people, processes, materials, and equipment. The fishbone diagram can help individuals and teams understand the root causes of the problem and identify potential solutions.

Another solution is to use a mind map to break down the problem into its components. This technique involves starting with the problem in the center of a piece of paper and then branching out to identify different factors that contribute to the problem. The mind map can help individuals and teams see the problem from different angles and identify potential solutions.

4. Use first principle thinking to question any assumptions you may have about the problem.

First principle thinking is a problem-solving approach that involves breaking down a problem into its fundamental components and questioning any assumptions made about it. This approach can be particularly useful when dealing with complex or novel problems, as it allows for a more thorough and objective analysis.

For example, consider the problem of transportation. An assumption might be that cars are the only way for people to get around. However, using first principle thinking, one might question this assumption and consider other modes of transportation, such as bikes, public transportation, or even walking. By challenging this assumption, new solutions may be discovered that were not previously considered.

Another example can be found in the development of electric vehicles. Initially, the assumption was that the cost of producing electric vehicles would be prohibitively expensive. However, using first principle thinking, innovators in the industry broke down the problem into its most basic components and discovered that advances in battery technology could significantly reduce the cost of production. This led to the development of more affordable electric vehicles, which are now becoming increasingly popular.

In summary, first principle thinking is a valuable problem-solving approach that can help identify new solutions by questioning assumptions and breaking down problems into their most basic components.

5. Gather as much information as possible about the problem, including data and research from multiple sources.

Gathering information is crucial in problem-solving as it helps in gaining a better understanding of the problem and its root causes. It allows us to identify trends, patterns, and other important information that can help in generating potential solutions.

For instance, in the healthcare industry, data gathering has played a significant role in improving healthcare outcomes. A study published in the Journal of Medical Systems found that the use of electronic health records (EHRs) has enabled the collection of large amounts of data, which can be analyzed to identify gaps in care delivery and improve patient outcomes. The study also found that the use of EHRs has increased patient satisfaction, improved care coordination, and reduced medical errors.

In another example, the city of Chicago used data gathering to identify areas with high rates of lead poisoning in children. By analyzing data on blood lead levels in children, the city was able to target resources and interventions to the neighborhoods with the highest rates of lead poisoning, resulting in a significant reduction in lead poisoning rates.

To gather information, various methods can be used such as conducting surveys, reviewing literature, conducting interviews, and using data analytics tools. It is important to ensure that the information gathered is from reliable sources and that it is relevant to the problem at hand.

6. Analyze the information objectively, using logic and reason to arrive at new insights.

When analyzing information objectively, it is important to evaluate the quality and relevance of the data to ensure that the insights drawn are accurate and reliable. This can be done by considering the source of the data, the sample size, and the methods used to collect and analyze it.

For example, if a study claims that a certain intervention is effective in treating a medical condition, it is important to evaluate the study design and sample size to ensure that the results are statistically significant and not biased.

As an example, let's consider the issue of climate change. According to NASA, 97% of climate scientists agree that climate-warming trends over the past century are very likely due to human activities. This conclusion is based on an objective analysis of multiple lines of evidence, including temperature records, ice core data, and satellite observations.

However, there are also dissenting voices in the scientific community who argue that climate change is not primarily caused by human activities. It is important to objectively evaluate the evidence and arguments put forth by both sides to arrive at an accurate understanding of the issue.

Overall, analyzing information objectively involves being open-minded, using critical thinking skills, and basing conclusions on solid evidence rather than personal biases or opinions.

7. Apply the additional problem-solving approaches, such as design thinking or Lean Six Sigma, to generate and test potential solutions.

Design thinking and Lean Six Sigma are two different problem-solving approaches that can be applied depending on the type of problem or challenge. Design thinking is a -centered approach that focuses on understanding the needs and preferences of the end-s and designing solutions that meet those needs. Lean Six Sigma, on the other hand, is a data-driven approach that focuses on improving the efficiency and quality of processes.

Let's take an example of a company that is experiencing a high rate of customer complaints about the quality of its products. In this case, a Lean Six Sigma approach would be appropriate to identify the root cause of the problem and make improvements to the manufacturing process. The company can use statistical tools to analyze the data and identify the areas of the process that need improvement.

On the other hand, if the challenge is to design a new product that meets the needs of a specific group, then a design thinking approach would be more appropriate. In this case, the company can use empathy and observation techniques to understand the needs and preferences of the group and generate ideas for potential solutions. The company can then prototype and test the solutions with the group to ensure that they meet their needs.

Both approaches can be complementary and can be used in combination to generate and test potential solutions. By applying both approaches, the company can ensure that the solutions are both -centered and data-driven, leading to more effective and efficient problem-solving.

8. *Evaluate each potential solution based on its feasibility, potential impact, and alignment with your values and goals.*

When evaluating potential solutions, it is important to consider their feasibility, potential impact, and alignment with your values and goals.

Feasibility refers to whether a solution is realistic and achievable given the available resources and constraints. For example, if a potential solution requires a large amount of funding that is not currently available, it may not be feasible.

Potential impact refers to the potential positive and negative effects a solution may have on the problem and other related factors. For example, a solution that addresses one aspect of a problem may have unintended consequences in other areas.

Alignment with values and goals refers to whether a solution is consistent with your personal or organizational values and long-term goals. For example, a solution that generates short-term profits but harms the environment may not align with an organization's sustainability goals.

Let's take the example of a company that wants to reduce its carbon footprint. One potential solution could be to switch to renewable energy sources for their manufacturing facilities. When evaluating this solution, the company should consider factors such as the feasibility of sourcing renewable energy, the potential impact on their manufacturing processes, and whether the solution aligns with their values and long-term goals of sustainability.

According to a report by the International Energy Agency (IEA), renewable energy sources such as solar and wind power are now the cheapest sources of electricity in most countries. This indicates that sourcing renewable energy may be feasible for the company. Additionally, transitioning to renewable energy could reduce the company's carbon emissions and align with their sustainability goals. However, the company would need to evaluate the potential impact of this solution on their manufacturing processes and whether any necessary changes could negatively impact their business operations.

In summary, evaluating potential solutions requires a careful consideration of feasibility, potential impact, and alignment with values and goals.

9. Test and validate your solutions through experiments or simulations.

Testing and validating potential solutions through experiments or simulations can be an effective way to determine their feasibility and potential impact. This allows you to test your ideas in a controlled environment before implementing them on a larger scale.

For example, if you are trying to improve the efficiency of a manufacturing process, you might create a simulation of the process to test different changes and improvements. You could also run small-scale experiments to test the impact of changes on productivity, quality, and cost.

Similarly, if you are designing a new product, you might create prototypes and conduct testing to validate the design and gather feedback for improvement. This iterative approach allows you to continuously refine and improve your solutions based on real-world feedback and data.

In the field of medicine, clinical trials are conducted to test new treatments or interventions for safety and effectiveness. These trials involve controlled experiments with human subjects to determine the potential impact of the treatment on the targeted health condition.

Overall, testing and validating potential solutions can help to identify potential flaws or issues, refine the solution, and ultimately increase the likelihood of success when implementing the solution on a larger scale.

10. Continuously iterate and improve upon the solution to refine it and make it even more effective.

Continuously iterating and improving upon the solution is an essential step in the problem-solving process to ensure that the solution remains effective and relevant. This step involves monitoring and evaluating the solution's performance and making necessary modifications to improve its effectiveness continually.

For example, consider the problem of reducing traffic congestion in a busy city. After conducting thorough research and analysis, a potential solution could be to implement a more extensive public transportation system. However, this solution may require constant monitoring and improvement to ensure that it is efficient and effective in reducing traffic congestion.

To continuously iterate and improve upon the solution, data can be collected and analyzed regularly to determine the system's effectiveness. The system's performance can be monitored by collecting information on the number of riders, peak usage times, and customer satisfaction levels.

Suppose the data collected reveals that the system is not meeting its goals or expectations. In that case, adjustments can be made to improve its effectiveness, such as increasing the frequency of buses or implementing additional routes in high-traffic areas.

In summary, continuously iterating and improving upon the solution ensures that it remains relevant and effective in addressing the problem at hand. This approach requires a willingness to adapt and make changes based on ongoing feedback and data analysis to ensure that the solution's impact is maximized.

CHAPTER 11

The Future Of First Principle Thinking: Exploring How This Mode Of Reasoning Might Evolve And Be Applied In The Years To Come.

1. Analyze the current trends in technology and how they may impact the way we approach problem-solving.

In recent years, technology has been rapidly advancing and revolutionizing the way we approach problem-solving. Here are some current trends in technology that are impacting problem-solving:

Artificial intelligence (AI) and machine learning: AI and machine learning are enabling computers to analyze vast amounts of data and make predictions, recommendations, and decisions without human intervention. This technology has the potential to revolutionize problem-solving by automating certain tasks and identifying patterns that humans might miss. For example, in healthcare, machine learning algorithms can help predict disease outbreaks and diagnose medical conditions.

Internet of Things (IoT): IoT refers to the network of physical devices, vehicles, home appliances, and other items embedded with sensors, software, and connectivity, enabling them to connect and exchange data. IoT has the potential to transform problem-solving by providing real-time data on how systems are functioning, allowing for proactive maintenance and repair. For example, IoT sensors can help identify and address potential problems with machines in a manufacturing plant before they cause significant downtime.

Blockchain technology: Blockchain is a decentralized, distributed ledger technology that provides secure and transparent record-keeping. Blockchain has the potential to transform problem-solving by creating a secure and transparent way to track and verify transactions, contracts, and other interactions. For example, in supply chain management, blockchain can help track the movement of goods from the source to the destination, reducing the risk of fraud and increasing transparency.

Virtual and augmented reality: Virtual and augmented reality technologies create immersive digital environments that can enhance problem-solving by providing new ways to visualize and interact with data. For example, in product design, virtual reality can be used to create realistic prototypes and test designs before physical production begins.

As technology continues to advance, it is crucial to stay informed about new developments and incorporate them into problem-solving strategies. It is also important to recognize that technology is not a panacea and that human judgment and creativity are still essential in effective problem-solving.

2. **Consider how first principle thinking may be applied to emerging fields such as biotechnology, nanotechnology, or artificial intelligence.**

First principle thinking, as a foundational approach to problem-solving, can be applied to emerging fields such as biotechnology, nanotechnology, and artificial intelligence. By breaking down complex problems into their fundamental components, first principle thinking can help identify novel solutions that leverage emerging technologies.

For example, in the field of biotechnology, first principle thinking can help identify key molecular interactions that can be targeted for the development of new therapeutics. By understanding the underlying biology of a disease, researchers can use first principle thinking to design and test new compounds that selectively modulate specific molecular targets. This approach has led to the development of new treatments for diseases such as cancer, diabetes, and autoimmune disorders.

In the field of nanotechnology, first principle thinking can be used to design and fabricate nanoscale materials with unique properties and functionalities. By understanding the underlying physics of nanoscale systems, researchers can use first principle thinking to design and optimize materials with tailored properties such as mechanical strength, electronic conductivity, and catalytic activity. This approach has led to the development of new materials for applications such as energy storage, catalysis, and sensors.

In the field of artificial intelligence, first principle thinking can be used to develop algorithms and models that are based on fundamental principles of mathematics and computer science. By understanding the underlying principles of machine learning and data analysis, researchers can use first principle thinking to develop new algorithms and models that can be applied to a wide range of applications such as natural language processing, computer vision, and robotics.

Overall, first principle thinking can provide a powerful framework for problem-solving in emerging fields such as biotechnology, nanotechnology, and artificial intelligence, enabling researchers to identify novel solutions and applications that leverage the latest technological advances.

3. **Explore how first principle thinking can be used to address global challenges such as climate change, pandemics, or poverty.**

First principle thinking can be a powerful tool for addressing global challenges such as climate change, pandemics, or poverty. By breaking down these complex problems into their most basic components and analyzing them objectively, we can identify new insights and potential solutions.

For example, in the case of climate change, first principle thinking can be used to identify the root causes of the problem and develop innovative solutions. Instead of relying on traditional methods of reducing greenhouse gas emissions, such as switching to renewable energy sources, we can explore new approaches such as carbon capture and storage, direct air capture, and geoengineering.

In the case of pandemics, first principle thinking can help us to better understand the underlying mechanisms of disease transmission and develop more effective strategies for prevention and treatment. By analyzing the basic components of viruses and their modes of transmission, we can develop new approaches such as mRNA vaccines, antiviral drugs, and novel methods of contact tracing and testing.

Similarly, first principle thinking can be applied to address poverty by breaking down the root causes of inequality and identifying innovative solutions. This might involve developing new models of economic development that prioritize sustainability, promoting education and training programs that provide skills and opportunities to underserved populations, or implementing new policies that address systemic inequalities such as discrimination and income inequality.

Overall, first principle thinking can be a valuable approach for addressing complex global challenges by encouraging us to think creatively, objectively, and outside the box. By analyzing problems at their most basic level and identifying new insights and solutions, we can make progress towards a more sustainable, equitable, and prosperous future.

4. Consider the impact of first principle thinking on various industries, such as healthcare, finance, or transportation.

First principle thinking can have a significant impact on various industries, including healthcare, finance, and transportation. Here are some examples:

Healthcare: First principle thinking can be applied to medical research to understand the fundamental mechanisms of diseases and develop new treatments. For example, researchers at the University of California, San Francisco used first principle thinking to identify a new drug target for tuberculosis. By analyzing the basic chemical reactions that occur in the bacterium that causes TB, they identified a specific enzyme that could be targeted by a new drug.

Finance: First principle thinking can be applied to financial modeling to develop more accurate predictions of market trends and investment opportunities. For example, the hedge fund Renaissance Technologies uses a first principle approach to develop quantitative trading strategies based on fundamental economic principles rather than relying on traditional market analysis.

Transportation: First principle thinking can be applied to the design of new transportation systems, such as hyperloop technology. Hyperloop technology is based on the first principle of reducing air resistance to increase speed and efficiency. By designing a vacuum-sealed tube and using magnetic levitation to reduce friction, hyperloop technology could revolutionize transportation by enabling high-speed travel over long distances.

Overall, first principle thinking has the potential to drive innovation and breakthroughs in a wide range of industries by challenging conventional wisdom and encouraging a more fundamental understanding of the underlying principles and mechanisms.

5. Explore how first principle thinking may be integrated into education and training programs to help develop critical thinking skills.

First principle thinking can be a valuable tool for developing critical thinking skills, which are essential for success in many fields. Integrating this approach into education and training programs can help students and professionals learn to approach problems in a more logical and innovative way.

There are several examples of how first principle thinking has been integrated into education and training programs. One example is the Stanford Design School's "d.school" program, which uses design thinking to teach problem-solving skills to students from a wide range of disciplines. The program emphasizes the importance of starting with a deep understanding of the problem and using first principle thinking to identify innovative solutions.

Another example is the "Breakthrough Innovation" program developed by the consulting firm Innosight, which teaches executives and entrepreneurs how to use first principle thinking to identify disruptive new business models. The program emphasizes the importance of questioning assumptions and using logic and reason to identify new opportunities.

In addition to these programs, many universities and schools have begun to integrate first principle thinking into their curricula. For example, the University of Waterloo in Canada has developed a course on first principles in engineering, which teaches students how to apply this approach to solve complex engineering problems.

The impact of integrating first principle thinking into education and training programs can be significant. By teaching students and professionals how to approach problems in a more logical and innovative way, these programs can help to foster a more creative and dynamic workforce. This, in turn, can lead to more innovative solutions to the challenges we face as a society.

Moreover, there is evidence that incorporating critical thinking skills in education can lead to better academic performance and achievement. A study by researchers at the University of Illinois found that students who participated in a critical thinking curriculum showed significant improvement in their writing and reasoning skills, as well as higher scores on standardized tests.

In conclusion, integrating first principle thinking into education and training programs can help to develop critical thinking skills and foster innovation in many fields. As technology and society continue to evolve, it is essential that we equip the next generation with the tools they need to tackle the complex challenges we face.

6. Consider how first principle thinking can be used in the development of public policy and governance.

First principle thinking can be a valuable approach in the development of public policy and governance as it allows policymakers to approach complex problems in a systematic and analytical manner. By breaking down problems into their fundamental components, policymakers can identify underlying assumptions and biases that may be limiting the effectiveness of current policies.

One example of the use of first principle thinking in public policy is the development of climate change policies. By analyzing the fundamental causes of climate change, such as greenhouse gas emissions, policymakers can develop policies that target the root cause of the problem. For example, a carbon tax could be implemented to incentivize companies to reduce their carbon emissions, or renewable energy subsidies could be introduced to encourage the use of cleaner energy sources.

Another example is the use of first principle thinking in healthcare policy. By analyzing the fundamental components of healthcare delivery, such as access to care, quality of care, and cost of care, policymakers can identify areas where the system can be improved. For example, policies could be implemented to increase access to care for underserved populations, or to improve the quality of care delivered by healthcare providers.

In terms of governance, first principle thinking can be used to analyze the fundamental components of democratic processes and identify areas where they can be improved. For example, policies could be implemented to increase access to voting, improve the accuracy and security of voting systems, or reduce the influence of money in politics.

Overall, the use of first principle thinking in public policy and governance can help policymakers develop more effective and sustainable policies that address the root causes of complex problems.

7. Explore the potential impact of first principle thinking on the way we approach ethical dilemmas.

First principle thinking can have a significant impact on the way we approach ethical dilemmas, particularly by helping us to identify and challenge underlying assumptions and biases. By breaking a problem down into its most basic components and analyzing them objectively, we can arrive at new insights and perspectives that may not have been apparent otherwise.

For example, let's consider the ethical dilemma of autonomous weapons. Autonomous weapons are robots that are programmed to make decisions and act on their own, without human intervention. This raises significant ethical concerns, particularly around the potential for unintended harm or loss of life.

Using first principle thinking, we can break down the problem into its most basic components and question our assumptions. For example, we can ask:

What are the specific ethical concerns related to autonomous weapons?
What are the potential benefits of autonomous weapons?
Are there alternative approaches to achieving those benefits that would be more ethical?
By analyzing the problem objectively and challenging our assumptions, we can arrive at new insights and perspectives that may help us to develop more effective and ethical solutions.

Overall, the integration of first principle thinking into ethical decision-making can help us to approach complex ethical dilemmas in a more systematic and rigorous way, leading to better outcomes for all involved.

8. Consider the impact of first principle thinking on the innovation process and how it may lead to new products and services.

First principle thinking can have a significant impact on the innovation process by encouraging individuals to question assumptions and identify underlying principles. This can lead to the development of new and innovative products and services that better address consumer needs. For example, Tesla Motors, led by entrepreneur Elon Musk, has used first principle thinking to innovate in the electric car industry.

Instead of accepting the existing limitations of battery technology, Musk and his team applied first principle thinking to identify the fundamental principles governing battery design and performance. They then used this understanding to develop new battery technology with higher energy density and longer lifetimes, which has enabled Tesla to produce electric vehicles with longer ranges and lower costs.

The impact of first principle thinking on innovation can also be seen in the technology sector, where companies like Apple and Google have used this approach to develop new products and services. For instance, Apple used first principle thinking to design the iPhone, which revolutionized the smartphone industry by combining the functionalities of multiple devices into a single, -friendly interface. Similarly, Google has used first principle thinking to develop innovative technologies like Google Maps and Google Glass.

Overall, the integration of first principle thinking into the innovation process can help organizations to create more value for their customers, increase their competitiveness, and drive long-term growth.

9. Analyze how first principle thinking can be used to drive organizational change and transformation.

First principle thinking can be a powerful tool for driving organizational change and transformation. By breaking down problems to their fundamental principles, organizations can identify new and innovative solutions that can transform their business models, processes, and operations.

For example, in the 1990s, Amazon CEO Jeff Bezos used first principle thinking to disrupt the traditional brick-and-mortar retail industry. He recognized that the high cost of real estate and overhead for physical stores was a major barrier to entry for new competitors. By starting with the first principles of what customers really wanted (low prices, a wide selection of products, and convenience), he was able to create a new business model that revolutionized the retail industry.

Similarly, Tesla CEO Elon Musk used first principle thinking to develop a new battery technology that could power electric vehicles for longer distances. Rather than accepting the limitations of existing battery technology, Musk and his team broke down the problem to its fundamental principles and identified new materials and manufacturing processes that could significantly improve battery performance. This innovation has transformed the electric vehicle market and helped to accelerate the transition to clean energy.

To drive organizational change and transformation, companies can encourage the use of first principle thinking in problem-solving and decision-making processes. This can involve training employees on the principles of first principle thinking, creating a culture that encourages questioning assumptions, and providing resources and support for innovative projects that challenge the status quo.

In addition, organizations can use first principle thinking to identify new opportunities for growth and innovation. By breaking down problems to their fundamental principles, companies can identify unmet needs and develop new products and services that address those needs. This can help companies stay ahead of the competition and continue to innovate in a rapidly changing business environment.

Overall, first principle thinking can be a valuable tool for driving organizational change and transformation. By encouraging a culture of innovation and questioning assumptions, organizations can identify new solutions to complex problems and develop new opportunities for growth and success.

10. Consider the role of first principle thinking in shaping the future of society and civilization as a whole.

First principle thinking has the potential to play a significant role in shaping the future of society and civilization by enabling us to approach complex challenges in innovative and transformative ways. By breaking down problems into their most basic components and questioning assumptions, we can arrive at new insights and solutions that were previously unconsidered.

For example, first principle thinking can be applied to the challenge of sustainable energy production. Instead of simply improving existing renewable energy technologies, first principle thinking can lead to the development of entirely new approaches, such as fusion energy or artificial photosynthesis.

In the field of transportation, first principle thinking has already led to the development of innovative solutions, such as electric cars and hyperloop transport systems. These solutions have the potential to revolutionize the way we travel and significantly reduce carbon emissions.

Another area where first principle thinking can have a significant impact is in healthcare. By questioning assumptions about disease and treatment, researchers can develop new and more effective therapies. For example, the development of CRISPR gene editing technology was a result of first principle thinking applied to the fundamental mechanisms of genetics.

Overall, first principle thinking has the potential to drive innovation and transformation across many fields, from technology to healthcare to public policy. By encouraging critical thinking and questioning assumptions, we can find new and innovative solutions to the complex challenges facing our society and civilization.

CHAPTER 12

Critiques Of First Principle Thinking: Examining The Potential Downsides And Limitations Of This Way Of Thinking.

1. Analyze the potential limitations of first principle thinking, such as the difficulty in identifying and breaking down complex problems into their most basic components.

First principle thinking is a powerful problem-solving approach that can lead to breakthrough innovations and solutions. However, like any other approach, it has its limitations. One potential limitation is the difficulty in identifying and breaking down complex problems into their most basic components.

Some problems may be so complex and multifaceted that it may be challenging to identify the underlying principles or first principles that govern them. For example, the challenge of reducing global poverty is a complex problem that involves multiple factors, including economic systems, political structures, cultural norms, and individual behaviors. Breaking down this problem into its most basic components may be difficult and may require a deep understanding of multiple disciplines and fields.

Another potential limitation of first principle thinking is the risk of oversimplifying problems. In some cases, breaking down a problem into its most basic components may lead to an oversimplified view of the problem and may overlook critical nuances and complexities. For example, reducing greenhouse gas emissions is a complex problem that involves multiple factors, including energy consumption patterns, industrial processes, transportation systems, and land use. Oversimplifying this problem by focusing solely on one or two factors may lead to suboptimal solutions.

To address these limitations, it may be necessary to complement first principle thinking with other problem-solving approaches, such as systems thinking, design thinking, or Lean Six Sigma. These approaches can help identify and address the complex interdependencies and interactions between different factors and components of a problem. Additionally, it may be useful to collaborate with experts and stakeholders from multiple fields and disciplines to gain a holistic understanding of the problem and its underlying principles.

In conclusion, while first principle thinking is a powerful problem-solving approach, it has its limitations, particularly in dealing with complex problems. By complementing first principle thinking with other approaches and collaborating with experts and stakeholders, we can develop more comprehensive and effective solutions to complex problems.

2. Consider the potential bias and subjectivity in the initial assumptions made during the first principle thinking process.

One of the potential limitations of first principle thinking is the bias and subjectivity that can be introduced during the initial assumption-making stage. The assumptions made during the problem-solving process can significantly impact the outcome and the effectiveness of the solution generated.

For example, if the problem being addressed is the gender pay gap, the initial assumption made about the cause of the gap can significantly impact the solutions generated. If the assumption made is that the gender pay gap is due to women not negotiating their salaries as effectively as men, the solution generated may focus on providing negotiation training to women. However, if the assumption made is that the gender pay gap is due to systemic discrimination, the solution generated may focus on policy changes that address discrimination in the workplace.

To overcome this limitation, it is essential to challenge and question assumptions rigorously, especially during the initial stages of the problem-solving process. Additionally, involving a diverse group of individuals with different backgrounds, experiences, and perspectives can help identify and address potential biases and subjectivity in the assumptions made.

Data analysis and research can also help reduce the impact of bias and subjectivity on the problem-solving process. By relying on data and evidence, rather than assumptions and opinions, it is possible to generate solutions that are objective and effective.

In conclusion, while bias and subjectivity are potential limitations of first principle thinking, they can be overcome through rigorous questioning and challenging of assumptions, involvement of diverse perspectives, and reliance on data and evidence.

3. Examine the potential for over-reliance on first principle thinking to lead to analysis paralysis or a lack of creativity and innovation.

While first principle thinking is a valuable problem-solving approach, it's important to acknowledge its potential limitations. One potential limitation is the risk of analysis paralysis, where the problem is broken down into such basic components that no progress is made towards a solution.

Another potential limitation is over-reliance on first principle thinking, which could lead to a lack of creativity and innovation. First principle thinking can be very effective at identifying and solving problems, but it's not always the best approach for generating new ideas or thinking outside the box. In these cases, it may be necessary to supplement first principle thinking with other problem-solving approaches such as design thinking or brainstorming.

Furthermore, first principle thinking relies on assumptions that are made at the beginning of the problem-solving process. These assumptions can be biased or subjective, leading to a flawed analysis and solution. It's important to acknowledge and challenge these assumptions to ensure that the solution is as objective and unbiased as possible.

One way to address these limitations is to incorporate a variety of problem-solving approaches into the process. By combining first principle thinking with other approaches, it's possible to overcome the limitations of each and arrive at a more comprehensive and effective solution. Additionally, regularly reviewing and testing the assumptions made during the problem-solving process can help to minimize bias and ensure that the analysis remains objective.

4. Explore the potential for first principle thinking to overlook important contextual factors or to be insufficiently sensitive to cultural or social dynamics.

First principle thinking can be a powerful problem-solving approach, but it has some limitations. One potential limitation is that it can overlook important contextual factors or be insufficiently sensitive to cultural or social dynamics.

Contextual factors and cultural considerations can play a significant role in shaping problems and solutions. Failure to account for these factors can lead to incomplete or ineffective solutions. First principle thinking may not always be sufficient in addressing these challenges, and may need to be supplemented by other problem-solving approaches.

For example, consider the challenge of improving access to healthcare in rural areas. A first principle thinking approach might focus on identifying the fundamental needs and constraints of the healthcare system, such as the availability of medical professionals, infrastructure, and funding. However, without considering the specific cultural and social dynamics of the rural area, this approach may overlook important factors that affect healthcare access, such as the role of community health workers, traditional healers, or cultural beliefs about healthcare.

To address this limitation, it may be helpful to incorporate other problem-solving approaches, such as design thinking or human-centered design, which prioritize empathy and understanding of s and their contexts. These approaches can help to identify and address cultural and social dynamics that may not be captured by a purely first principle thinking approach.

In summary, while first principle thinking can be a powerful problem-solving approach, it is important to recognize its limitations and to supplement it with other approaches as necessary to ensure that solutions are effective and appropriate for the specific context.

5. Analyze the potential for first principle thinking to be overly reductionist or to oversimplify complex problems.

First principle thinking can be seen as a reductionist approach, which involves breaking down complex problems into their most basic components. While this can be a useful tool, there is the potential for oversimplification and reductionism, which can lead to overlooking important contextual factors and complexities.

For example, in healthcare, first principle thinking may be useful in developing new treatments or drugs by understanding the underlying biological mechanisms of a disease. However, this approach may not fully capture the complexity of social and cultural factors that influence health outcomes, such as access to healthcare, socioeconomic status, and cultural beliefs about health.

To mitigate the potential for oversimplification, it is important to use first principle thinking in conjunction with other problem-solving approaches and to incorporate diverse perspectives and expertise. It is also important to remain open to the complexity and nuance of a problem and to continuously re-evaluate and iterate solutions based on new information and feedback.

Additionally, the use of technology such as machine learning and artificial intelligence can help to identify patterns and insights that may be difficult to identify through first principle thinking alone. By combining multiple approaches and perspectives, we can ensure a more comprehensive and nuanced understanding of complex problems.

6. **Consider the potential for first principle thinking to be time-consuming and resource-intensive, making it difficult to apply in real-world settings with tight deadlines or limited resources.**

First principle thinking, while a valuable problem-solving approach, can be time-consuming and resource-intensive, which can make it difficult to apply in real-world settings with tight deadlines or limited resources. This is because it involves breaking down complex problems into their most basic components and then building up solutions from there, which can be a time-consuming process. Additionally, identifying the most important first principles can also be difficult and require significant effort and resources.

However, there are strategies that can be employed to mitigate these limitations. One solution is to use a hybrid approach, combining first principle thinking with other problem-solving techniques to arrive at a solution. This can help to speed up the process and reduce the amount of resources required, while still taking advantage of the benefits of first principle thinking.

Another strategy is to prioritize the most important first principles and focus on those rather than trying to identify and address every single component of a complex problem. This can help to streamline the process and make it more efficient, while still ensuring that the most critical aspects of the problem are addressed.

Finally, using technology and automation can also help to speed up the first principle thinking process. For example, machine learning algorithms can be used to identify the most important first principles and suggest potential solutions based on that analysis. This can help to reduce the amount of time and resources required while still leveraging the power of first principle thinking.

In summary, while there are potential limitations to first principle thinking, there are also solutions that can be employed to mitigate these limitations and ensure that this problem-solving approach is still valuable in real-world settings with limited resources and tight deadlines.

7. **Explore the potential for first principle thinking to be challenging for individuals with limited expertise in a particular field or domain.**

First principle thinking can be challenging for individuals with limited expertise in a particular field or domain because it requires a deep understanding of the fundamental principles and underlying concepts of that field or domain. Without such knowledge, it may be difficult to identify the key assumptions or to break down complex problems into their most basic components. However, with proper training and education, individuals can develop the necessary expertise to apply first principle thinking effectively.

Studies have shown that education and training can significantly enhance an individual's problem-solving abilities. For example, a study conducted by the National Institute for Learning Outcomes Assessment found that students who participated in problem-based learning activities demonstrated a significant improvement in their critical thinking and problem-solving skills. Similarly, a study published in the Journal of the Academy of Business Education found that students who participated in a business simulation exercise demonstrated a significant improvement in their decision-making and problem-solving abilities.

To address the challenge of limited expertise, organizations can provide targeted training and education programs to help employees develop the necessary knowledge and skills to apply first principle thinking effectively. This can include providing access to online courses or workshops, offering mentorship or coaching programs, and encouraging employees to participate in cross-functional projects and teams to develop a more comprehensive understanding of different domains.

In addition, organizations can create a culture that encourages continuous learning and development, where employees are encouraged to seek out new knowledge and skills and are provided with opportunities for growth and development. By investing in education and training, organizations can ensure that their employees have the skills and knowledge necessary to apply first principle thinking effectively and to drive innovation and growth within the organization.

8. **Consider the potential for first principle thinking to be more effective in certain types of problems, such as those with clear cause-and-effect relationships, rather than in more complex, multi-dimensional challenges.**

First principle thinking is a powerful problem-solving approach that has been successfully applied in a variety of domains. However, it is important to acknowledge its potential limitations and recognize that it may not always be the best approach for every problem. One potential limitation of first principle thinking is that it may be more effective in certain types of problems than in others.

For example, first principle thinking may be more effective in problems with clear cause-and-effect relationships, where it is easier to identify and break down the underlying assumptions. In contrast, more complex, multi-dimensional problems may be more challenging to approach with a first principle thinking mindset. These types of problems may require a more holistic, systems thinking approach that takes into account the many interrelated factors that contribute to the problem.

One example of a problem that may be more challenging to approach with first principle thinking is climate change. Climate change is a complex and multi-dimensional challenge that involves many interrelated factors, including greenhouse gas emissions, land use, energy consumption, and global politics. While first principle thinking may be useful in breaking down some of the underlying assumptions related to these factors, it may not be sufficient to fully address the complex nature of the problem.

To address this limitation, it may be useful to combine first principle thinking with other problem-solving approaches, such as systems thinking or design thinking. By taking a more holistic approach that incorporates a range of problem-solving strategies, we can more effectively tackle complex challenges like climate change.

In conclusion, while first principle thinking is a powerful problem-solving approach, it is important to recognize its potential limitations and to approach problems with a range of problem-solving strategies. By combining first principle thinking with other approaches, we can more effectively tackle complex challenges and drive innovation in a variety of domains.

9. Analyze the potential for first principle thinking to be overly deterministic or to fail to account for uncertainty or unpredictability in complex systems.

One of the potential limitations of first principle thinking is its potential to be overly deterministic or fail to account for uncertainty or unpredictability in complex systems. This is particularly relevant in fields such as economics, climate science, and healthcare, where there are often many interacting variables and factors that can influence outcomes.

For example, in climate science, first principle thinking may lead to a focus on reducing carbon emissions as the key factor in mitigating climate change. While this is certainly an important factor, it may overlook the complex interactions between various factors such as land use, agriculture, and industrial processes, which can also contribute to greenhouse gas emissions and affect the climate system.

Similarly, in healthcare, first principle thinking may lead to a focus on identifying and treating specific disease pathways or biomarkers, while overlooking the complex interplay between genetics, environmental factors, and social determinants of health.

To address this limitation, it may be necessary to combine first principle thinking with other problem-solving approaches, such as scenario planning or systems thinking, to account for uncertainty and unpredictability in complex systems. These approaches can help to identify and explore a range of potential outcomes and factors that may influence them, allowing for a more nuanced and comprehensive understanding of the problem at hand.

Overall, while first principle thinking can be a powerful tool for problem-solving, it is important to recognize its limitations and to use it in combination with other approaches to ensure a more comprehensive and effective solution.

10. Consider the potential for first principle thinking to be less effective in collaborative or team-based settings, where multiple perspectives and expertise are required.

First principle thinking can be challenging to implement in collaborative or team-based settings, as it requires a high degree of individual thinking and may not easily integrate with other problem-solving approaches. Moreover, the emphasis on individual thinking and breaking down problems into basic components may overlook the importance of collaboration and teamwork in addressing complex challenges.

According to a study by the National Bureau of Economic Research, teamwork and collaboration are becoming increasingly important in modern workplaces. The study found that the share of work performed by teams has increased by 50% in the past 20 years, and the use of teams is expected to continue to grow in the future. This trend is particularly true in industries such as technology and healthcare, where complex problems require multiple perspectives and areas of expertise.

To overcome the limitations of first principle thinking in team settings, it is essential to create a collaborative environment that fosters open communication and encourages diverse perspectives. This can be achieved by implementing structured brainstorming sessions or group problem-solving activities that encourage team members to share their ideas and perspectives.

Another way to integrate first principle thinking into team-based problem-solving is to use it in conjunction with other approaches, such as design thinking or agile methodology. By combining different approaches, teams can leverage the strengths of each method to develop innovative and effective solutions to complex challenges.

Overall, while first principle thinking may have limitations in team-based settings, it can still be a valuable tool for individual team members to use in their own problem-solving processes. By combining this approach with collaborative techniques, teams can effectively leverage the strengths of each member to develop innovative and effective solutions to complex challenges.

CHAPTER 13

Cultivating A First Principle Mindset: Tips And Exercises For Developing A First Principle Mindset And Making It A Habit.

1. Practice breaking down complex problems into their fundamental components by asking "why" questions to get to the root cause of the issue.

Breaking down complex problems into their fundamental components is an essential part of problem-solving. One effective way to do this is by using the "5 Whys" technique, which involves asking "why" questions repeatedly until the root cause of the problem is identified.

For example, let's say a company is experiencing a high rate of employee turnover. By asking "why" repeatedly, the company can uncover the root cause of the problem.

Why are employees leaving? Because they are unhappy with their job.
Why are they unhappy with their job? Because they don't feel valued by the company.
Why don't they feel valued by the company? Because their supervisors don't provide enough feedback or recognition.
Why don't supervisors provide enough feedback or recognition? Because they are overloaded with other tasks and don't have time to focus on employee development.
Why are they overloaded with other tasks? Because there is a lack of communication and coordination between departments.
By using this technique, the company can identify the root cause of the problem and develop targeted solutions to address it.

According to a survey conducted by McKinsey, 90% of executives agree that breaking down complex problems into smaller parts is critical for success. Additionally, 70% of executives believe that problem-solving is a critical skill for their organization to succeed.

Overall, practicing the skill of breaking down complex problems into their fundamental components can lead to more effective problem-solving and better outcomes for individuals and organizations.

2. Challenge assumptions and biases by asking whether they can be logically derived from first principles or if they are based on external factors.

Challenging assumptions and biases is a critical aspect of first principle thinking. Here are some ways to apply this in practice:

Question everything: A key aspect of challenging assumptions and biases is to question everything. This means asking questions such as "Why do we believe this?" and "What evidence supports this assumption?" This can help identify any biases or assumptions that may be influencing our thinking.

Use data to support your assumptions: When making assumptions, it is important to ensure that they are based on data and evidence. This helps to reduce the influence of bias and ensures that our assumptions are grounded in reality.

Consider alternative perspectives: To challenge our assumptions, it is important to consider alternative perspectives. This means seeking out diverse viewpoints and opinions to help identify any biases or assumptions that we may have overlooked.

Be open to changing your mind: Finally, it is important to be open to changing your mind based on new information or evidence. This helps to ensure that our thinking is always grounded in reality and not influenced by bias or assumptions.

For example, let's consider a company that has been experiencing declining sales. Instead of assuming that the problem is due to poor marketing or a lack of innovation, first principle thinking would involve breaking down the problem into its fundamental components and asking "Why are sales declining?" By challenging assumptions and biases, the company may identify that the real issue is due to a lack of understanding of their target audience or poor customer service. By addressing these root causes, the company may be able to improve sales and achieve long-term success.

3. Develop the ability to distinguish between observations, conclusions, and assumptions, and evaluate each on their own merits.

Developing the ability to distinguish between observations, conclusions, and assumptions is a key aspect of first principle thinking. Observations are facts that are directly observable and can be verified, while conclusions are inferences drawn from those observations. Assumptions, on the other hand, are beliefs or ideas that are taken for granted without necessarily being based on evidence.

One way to develop this skill is through critical thinking exercises, such as evaluating arguments and identifying logical fallacies. For example, a study published in the Journal of Educational Psychology found that students who participated in a critical thinking program improved their ability to identify fallacious arguments and make sound judgments (Halpern, 1998).

Another approach is to practice reframing assumptions as hypotheses that can be tested through experimentation or further analysis. This can help to uncover biases and uncover new insights. For example, the scientific method involves forming hypotheses based on first principles and then testing those hypotheses through experiments or observation.

Overall, developing the ability to distinguish between observations, conclusions, and assumptions can help to improve decision-making, problem-solving, and critical thinking skills.

4. Cultivate an openness to new information and perspectives, and be willing to revise your assumptions and beliefs based on new evidence.
Cultivating an openness to new information and perspectives is an important aspect of first principle thinking, as it allows individuals to challenge their assumptions and biases and refine their understanding of complex problems. A study published in the Journal of Experimental Psychology found that individuals who are more open to new experiences and information are better able to solve complex problems and generate creative solutions.

One way to cultivate openness is through exposure to diverse perspectives and experiences. Research has shown that diversity of thought and experience can lead to better problem-solving and innovation. For example, a study published in Harvard Business Review found that companies with more diverse leadership teams were more innovative and had higher financial performance than less diverse teams.

Another way to cultivate openness is to actively seek out feedback and constructive criticism. Research has shown that individuals who are open to feedback and willing to learn from their mistakes are more likely to be successful in their careers. In addition, seeking out feedback can help individuals identify blind spots and refine their thinking.

Overall, cultivating an openness to new information and perspectives requires a willingness to challenge one's own assumptions and beliefs, actively seek out diverse perspectives and experiences, and be open to constructive feedback and criticism. By doing so, individuals can improve their ability to think critically and creatively, and generate innovative solutions to complex problems.

5. Practice thinking critically and systematically, and avoid making hasty judgments or decisions based on incomplete information.

Thinking critically and systematically is essential for making informed decisions and solving complex problems. Here are some statistics and examples that highlight the importance of this skill:

According to a study by the Foundation for Critical Thinking, 69% of employers rated critical thinking as an essential skill for new hires.

In a survey by the Association of American Colleges and Universities, 93% of employers stated that a demonstrated capacity to think critically, communicate clearly, and solve complex problems is more important than an applicant's undergraduate major.

One example of the importance of critical thinking is the 1986 Space Shuttle Challenger disaster, which resulted from a flawed decision-making process. Engineers and managers ignored data indicating that the cold temperatures on the day of the launch would affect the O-ring seals on the shuttle's solid rocket boosters. This failure to think critically and systematically led to the loss of seven lives.

To cultivate critical thinking skills, individuals can practice questioning assumptions, examining evidence, and considering alternative perspectives. They can also develop a structured approach to problem-solving, such as the scientific method or the DMAIC process used in Six Sigma. By taking a systematic approach and avoiding hasty judgments, individuals can improve their ability to make informed decisions and solve complex problems.

6. Develop your analytical and reasoning skills by practicing with puzzles, riddles, or logic games.

Engaging in puzzles, riddles, or logic games can be an effective way to develop analytical and reasoning skills, which are critical for applying first principle thinking. According to a study published in the journal Intelligence, individuals who regularly engage in these types of activities tend to have higher cognitive abilities, including better problem-solving skills and improved working memory (Chuderski, 2014).

One example of a logic game that can help develop first principle thinking skills is Sudoku. In order to solve a Sudoku puzzle, individuals must break down a complex problem into its fundamental components and systematically work through each step to arrive at a solution. This process requires critical thinking and logical reasoning, both of which are key components of first principle thinking.

Other examples of logic games that can help develop first principle thinking skills include crossword puzzles, chess, and brainteasers. By regularly engaging in these types of activities, individuals can improve their ability to break down complex problems, analyze information, and arrive at logical conclusions.

In addition to these games, there are also a variety of online courses and training programs that can help individuals develop their analytical and reasoning skills. For example, Coursera offers a course on critical thinking and problem-solving skills, which teaches individuals how to break down complex problems, evaluate evidence, and arrive at logical conclusions. By taking advantage of these resources, individuals can improve their ability to apply first principle thinking in a variety of contexts.

7. Cultivate creativity by practicing brainstorming techniques, exploring new ideas, and thinking outside the box.

Cultivating creativity is an important part of the first principle thinking process as it allows individuals to explore new ideas and solutions to complex problems. Brainstorming is a popular technique used to generate creative ideas in a group setting. A study conducted by researchers at the University of Oklahoma found that group brainstorming sessions can be more effective at generating a larger number of ideas compared to individual brainstorming sessions.

Another way to cultivate creativity is by exploring new ideas and concepts. This can be done by exposing oneself to new experiences, reading books and articles, and engaging with people from diverse backgrounds. Research has shown that exposure to diverse perspectives can enhance creativity and problem-solving skills.

Lastly, thinking outside the box is an important skill to cultivate when engaging in first principle thinking. This involves challenging assumptions and exploring unconventional solutions to problems. A study conducted by researchers at the University of Illinois found that individuals who engaged in unconventional thinking were more likely to come up with innovative solutions to problems.

In conclusion, developing creativity is an important part of first principle thinking, and can be cultivated through brainstorming techniques, exposure to diverse perspectives, and thinking outside the box.

8. **Learn from past experiences and apply lessons learned to new situations.**

Learning from past experiences and applying the lessons learned is a critical component of first principle thinking. By examining past successes and failures, individuals can identify patterns and use this knowledge to make better decisions in the future.

For example, a study by the University of Michigan found that organizations that actively learn from their past experiences are more likely to innovate and adapt to changing circumstances. In the study, researchers found that companies that had a culture of learning from past experiences were more likely to introduce new products, improve their production processes, and increase their market share.

Furthermore, in the field of medicine, doctors are encouraged to learn from past cases to improve patient outcomes. For example, a study published in the Journal of Clinical Oncology found that by analyzing past cases of chemotherapy-induced nausea and vomiting, doctors were able to identify best practices and reduce the incidence of these side effects in future patients.

In addition, learning from past experiences can be applied to personal growth and development. By reflecting on past successes and failures, individuals can identify patterns and behaviors that contributed to their success or impeded their progress. This can lead to increased self-awareness and improved decision-making skills in the future.

Overall, learning from past experiences is a crucial aspect of first principle thinking and can lead to improved decision-making and innovation in various fields.

9. Seek out diverse perspectives and feedback to challenge your assumptions and broaden your understanding.

Seeking diverse perspectives and feedback is essential to ensuring that first principle thinking is not biased or incomplete. When working on complex problems, it's important to consider multiple viewpoints to arrive at the best possible solution. Studies have shown that diverse teams outperform homogeneous teams when it comes to problem-solving and decision-making.

For example, a study by McKinsey & Company found that companies in the top quartile for gender diversity were 21% more likely to experience above-average profitability than companies in the bottom quartile. Similarly, companies in the top quartile for ethnic and cultural diversity were 33% more likely to outperform their peers on profitability.

To seek out diverse perspectives and feedback, you can engage with people from different backgrounds and experiences, seek out feedback from colleagues with different skill sets and areas of expertise, and actively seek out viewpoints that challenge your assumptions. This can be done through collaborative brainstorming sessions, peer review processes, and cross-functional team collaborations.

Another effective approach is to seek out feedback from external sources, such as customers, stakeholders, or experts in the field. This can help to identify blind spots and gaps in your thinking, and can lead to new insights and perspectives that can improve the quality of your analysis.

In summary, seeking out diverse perspectives and feedback is essential for effective first principle thinking. It can help to identify biases and blind spots, and can lead to better problem-solving and decision-making.

10. Practice applying first principle thinking in real-world situations, and reflect on your successes and failures to continue refining your approach.

Practice is key to mastering any skill, and first principle thinking is no exception. Here are some examples of how to apply first principle thinking in real-world situations:

Elon Musk, founder of SpaceX, used first principle thinking to challenge the traditional approach to rocket design. Rather than relying on existing materials and designs, he broke down the problem into its fundamental components and used physics principles to create a more efficient and cost-effective rocket.

In the field of medicine, doctors and researchers use first principle thinking to understand the underlying biological mechanisms of diseases and develop new treatments. By breaking down the problem into its fundamental components and understanding the root cause of a disease, they can develop targeted therapies that are more effective and have fewer side effects.

In the business world, companies use first principle thinking to identify new markets and develop innovative products. By breaking down customer needs and desires into their most basic components, companies can develop solutions that address underlying problems and create new value for customers.

To continue refining your first principle thinking approach, it's important to reflect on your successes and failures. Consider the following questions:

Did you effectively break down the problem into its fundamental components?
Did you challenge your assumptions and biases?
Did you apply a systematic and logical approach to your analysis?
Did you consider multiple perspectives and feedback?
By continuously evaluating your approach and seeking feedback, you can improve your first principle thinking skills and apply them more effectively in a variety of situations.

CHAPTER 14

Debating And Challenging Assumptions Through First Principle Thinking: How To Use First Principle Thinking To Question The Status Quo.

1. Identify the assumptions underlying the status quo or conventional wisdom and question their validity.

Identifying and questioning the assumptions underlying the status quo or conventional wisdom is an important aspect of critical thinking and can lead to new insights and perspectives. This involves examining long-held beliefs or assumptions and challenging them to see if they hold up to scrutiny. Here are some examples:

Example 1: The assumption that high school students should follow a traditional four-year college track.

According to the National Center for Education Statistics, in 2018, 66.2% of high school graduates enrolled in college within a year of graduation. However, the assumption that all students should follow a traditional four-year college track is being increasingly challenged, as many students are finding that alternative pathways, such as vocational training or apprenticeships, can lead to rewarding and well-paying careers. By questioning this assumption, educators and policymakers are exploring new options for students that may better match their interests and skills.

Example 2: The assumption that work should be done in an office or workplace.

The COVID-19 pandemic has challenged the assumption that work should be done in a traditional office or workplace. With many companies shifting to remote work, employees are finding that they can be just as productive, if not more so, working from home. This has led to discussions about the future of work and the potential for more flexible and remote work arrangements in the long term.

Solution: In order to challenge assumptions underlying the status quo, it is important to critically evaluate the evidence and data supporting them, and to be open to new perspectives and ideas. This can involve seeking out diverse opinions and experiences, conducting research and analysis, and experimenting with new approaches or strategies. By questioning assumptions and challenging the status quo, individuals and organizations can open up new possibilities and pathways for growth and innovation.

2. Gather data and evidence to evaluate the assumptions and determine whether they are based on fact or opinion.

When challenging assumptions, gathering data and evidence is crucial in order to evaluate their validity. This can be achieved through various means such as surveys, experiments, and observational studies. Here are some examples:

In the early 1900s, it was widely assumed that women were not suited for higher education and should focus on domestic duties. However, in 1907, a study was conducted at the University of Iowa that compared the academic performance of men and women in college. The results showed that women were just as capable as men in academic achievement. This challenged the assumption that women were intellectually inferior and paved the way for women's higher education.

In the field of medicine, assumptions about the effectiveness of certain treatments or medications are constantly being challenged through clinical trials and studies. For example, a study published in 2020 in the New England Journal of Medicine found that hydroxychloroquine, a drug that was initially thought to be effective in treating COVID-19, did not provide any significant benefit to patients with the disease.

Assumptions about consumer preferences and behavior can also be challenged through market research. For example, a study conducted by Nielsen in 2019 found that consumers are increasingly prioritizing sustainability and are willing to pay more for products that are environmentally friendly. This challenged the assumption that consumers only care about price and convenience.

In each of these examples, data and evidence were used to challenge assumptions and reveal new insights. This highlights the importance of gathering objective data and conducting rigorous analysis when challenging assumptions.

3. Analyze the logic behind the assumptions and identify any flaws or inconsistencies.

Analyzing the logic behind assumptions is a critical aspect of critical thinking, which is the process of evaluating information and arguments to make informed judgments. When evaluating assumptions, it is important to assess their logical consistency and coherence, as well as their plausibility based on available evidence.

For example, let's say that a company assumes that increasing employee salaries will lead to increased productivity. To analyze the logic behind this assumption, one might consider the following questions:

What is the theoretical basis for this assumption? Are there empirical studies or data that support this claim?
Is there evidence that higher salaries lead to increased motivation and job satisfaction, which in turn leads to increased productivity?

Are there any counterexamples or alternative explanations for why increasing salaries might not lead to increased productivity?

By analyzing the logic behind assumptions, individuals can develop a more nuanced understanding of complex issues and make better-informed decisions. It can also help identify areas where further research or investigation may be necessary to evaluate the validity of certain assumptions.

There are many statistical tools and methods that can be used to analyze the logic behind assumptions, including hypothesis testing, regression analysis, and data visualization. These methods can help individuals identify patterns and relationships in data, assess the strength of evidence, and evaluate the validity of assumptions.

4. Challenge assumptions by asking "why" questions to get to the root cause of the issue.

Challenging assumptions by asking "why" questions is a key aspect of first principle thinking. This approach can be particularly effective when dealing with complex problems where assumptions are often embedded in the status quo or conventional wisdom. By questioning assumptions, we can identify potential flaws or biases that may be limiting our understanding of the problem.

For example, in the early 20th century, it was widely assumed that it was impossible for humans to run a mile in under four minutes. However, in 1954, Roger Bannister broke this assumption by running a mile in 3 minutes and 59.4 seconds. This achievement was not only a physical feat, but also a mental one that challenged the assumption that such a feat was impossible.

Similarly, in the business world, assumptions about what makes a successful product or business model can limit innovation and growth. By questioning these assumptions, companies can identify new opportunities and competitive advantages. For example, Airbnb challenged the assumption that the hotel industry was the only option for travelers, and disrupted the industry by offering a new platform for home-sharing.

To effectively challenge assumptions, it is important to ask "why" questions to get to the root cause of the issue. For example, if the assumption is that a particular strategy is the only way to achieve a goal, we can ask why that strategy is believed to be the only option, and explore alternative approaches.

Overall, challenging assumptions is a powerful tool for first principle thinking that can lead to breakthroughs and innovation. By questioning assumptions and examining the logic behind them, we can identify new opportunities and approaches to complex problems.

5. Consider alternative perspectives and viewpoints to broaden your understanding and challenge your assumptions.

Considering alternative perspectives and viewpoints is an essential part of challenging assumptions and broadening one's understanding of a particular issue. Here are some examples of how considering alternative perspectives has led to breakthroughs in various fields:

Medicine: In the mid-20th century, it was widely assumed that stomach ulcers were caused by stress and poor diet. However, two Australian researchers, Barry Marshall and Robin Warren, challenged this assumption by proposing that stomach ulcers were actually caused by bacteria. They faced skepticism from the medical community, but through their persistence and evidence-based research, they ultimately proved their hypothesis and revolutionized the treatment of stomach ulcers.

Science: For centuries, it was widely assumed that the universe was static and unchanging. However, in the early 20th century, astronomers such as Edwin Hubble began to gather evidence that the universe was actually expanding. This challenged the existing assumptions and ultimately led to the development of the Big Bang theory of the universe's origins.

Business: In the early 2000s, the music industry assumed that consumers would never pay for digital music and attempted to combat piracy through lawsuits and digital rights management software. However, companies such as Apple and Spotify challenged this assumption by developing -friendly and affordable digital music platforms that ultimately transformed the music industry.

These examples highlight the importance of considering alternative perspectives and challenging assumptions. By doing so, individuals and organizations can gain new insights and develop innovative solutions to long-standing problems.

To actively consider alternative perspectives, one can engage in activities such as seeking out diverse viewpoints, conducting research and gathering evidence, and engaging in open and respectful dialogue with others. Additionally, taking a growth mindset approach and being open to the possibility of being wrong can help individuals and organizations overcome cognitive biases and improve their ability to challenge assumptions.

6. Use logic and reasoning to evaluate different arguments and positions.

Using logic and reasoning to evaluate different arguments and positions is a critical thinking skill that can help individuals identify and challenge faulty assumptions. This approach involves examining the evidence and logic behind different claims and evaluating them based on their soundness and validity.

For example, in a study conducted by Stanford University researchers, participants were presented with information about a new skin cream product. The information included a positive review from a well-known celebrity, as well as a negative review from a consumer group. Participants who were trained in logical reasoning were more likely to recognize the flaws in both the positive and negative reviews and come to a more accurate conclusion about the product's effectiveness.

In another example, during the 2016 US presidential election, there were numerous arguments and positions put forth by candidates and their supporters. Using logic and reasoning, individuals could evaluate these arguments based on their soundness and validity, rather than relying solely on emotional appeal or personal bias.

To improve this skill, individuals can practice analyzing arguments and identifying the evidence and logic behind them. They can also learn to recognize common fallacies, such as ad hominem attacks or appeals to emotion, and avoid relying on them in their own arguments.

Solutions for developing this skill include taking courses in logic or critical thinking, practicing with logic puzzles and exercises, and seeking out diverse perspectives and feedback to challenge one's own assumptions and beliefs.

7. Evaluate the potential consequences of different assumptions and positions.

Evaluating the potential consequences of different assumptions and positions is an important aspect of first principle thinking. It involves considering the potential outcomes or impacts of different assumptions and positions before making a decision. This can help to avoid unintended consequences and ensure that the decision made is in line with the desired outcome.

For example, in the field of public policy, the consequences of different assumptions and positions can have a significant impact on society. One study found that the implementation of a tax on sugar-sweetened beverages could have a significant impact on obesity rates and save billions in healthcare costs. However, there are also concerns about the potential economic impact on the beverage industry and the regressive nature of the tax, which could disproportionately affect low-income individuals (Rettenmaier & Wang, 2016).

Another example can be seen in the context of environmental policy. The assumption that climate change is caused by human activity has led to the implementation of policies aimed at reducing greenhouse gas emissions. However, some argue that these policies could have negative economic consequences, such as increased energy costs and decreased economic growth (Lomborg, 2015).

To evaluate the potential consequences of different assumptions and positions, it is important to gather and analyze data, consider the perspectives of different stakeholders, and use logic and reasoning to evaluate the potential outcomes. One solution to help evaluate the potential consequences of different assumptions and positions is the use of scenario planning, which involves developing different scenarios based on different assumptions and evaluating the potential outcomes of each scenario. This can help to identify potential risks and opportunities and ensure that decisions are made based on a thorough analysis of the potential consequences.

8. Identify biases and assumptions that may be clouding your own judgment and work to overcome them.

Confirmation bias is a common cognitive bias that can impact decision-making and lead to faulty assumptions. Confirmation bias occurs when people seek out information that supports their pre-existing beliefs and ignore or discount information that contradicts them.

One solution to overcoming confirmation bias is to actively seek out diverse perspectives and information that challenges your assumptions. This can help broaden your understanding and expose you to new ideas and information that may have been overlooked.

Another solution is to engage in introspection and self-reflection to identify your own biases and assumptions. By acknowledging and addressing these biases, you can work to overcome them and make more objective and rational decisions.

For example, in a study published in the Journal of Personality and Social Psychology, researchers found that people who were more likely to engage in introspection were less likely to exhibit confirmation bias in their decision-making. Similarly, a study published in the Journal of Experimental Psychology found that encouraging people to consider alternative viewpoints and arguments led to more balanced and reasoned decision-making.

In conclusion, by actively seeking out diverse perspectives, engaging in introspection, and evaluating the potential consequences of different assumptions, individuals can work to identify and overcome biases and make more rational and objective decisions.

9. Engage in open and respectful dialogue with others to explore different perspectives and challenge assumptions.

Engaging in open and respectful dialogue with others is an essential skill for first principle thinking, as it allows individuals to explore different perspectives and challenge assumptions. Here are some examples, statistics, and solutions that elaborate on this topic:

Statistics: In a study by Harvard Business Review, teams that engaged in open and respectful dialogue performed better and had more innovative ideas than those that did not.

Live examples: One example of the power of open dialogue is the civil rights movement in the United States. Through peaceful protests, sit-ins, and other forms of activism, civil rights activists engaged in open dialogue with those in power to challenge assumptions about race and discrimination. Their efforts led to significant changes in laws and attitudes.

Solutions: To engage in open and respectful dialogue with others, it's important to approach the conversation with an open mind, actively listen to what others have to say, and avoid becoming defensive or confrontational. Additionally, individuals should strive to maintain a level of respect and civility throughout the conversation, even when disagreements arise.

Overall, engaging in open and respectful dialogue is an important component of first principle thinking, as it helps individuals broaden their understanding and challenge assumptions in a constructive and productive way.

10. Remain open-minded and willing to revise your own assumptions based on new evidence or perspectives.

Remaining open-minded and willing to revise your assumptions based on new evidence or perspectives is essential for effective first principle thinking. This allows for a more comprehensive understanding of a problem or situation and the ability to make informed decisions.

One example of the importance of being open-minded and willing to revise assumptions can be seen in the field of medicine. In the mid-20th century, it was assumed that stomach ulcers were caused by stress and poor diet. However, in the 1980s, two Australian researchers, Barry Marshall and Robin Warren, challenged this assumption by suggesting that stomach ulcers were caused by a bacterium called Helicobacter pylori. Despite facing significant resistance from the medical community, Marshall and Warren continued their research and eventually proved that their hypothesis was correct. This discovery led to a complete shift in how stomach ulcers are treated, from solely managing symptoms with antacids to curing the underlying bacterial infection with antibiotics.

In business, being open-minded and willing to revise assumptions can lead to innovative solutions and new opportunities. For example, in the early 2000s, the traditional taxi industry assumed that customers would always prefer the convenience and safety of traditional taxi services over ride-hailing services. However, companies like Uber and Lyft challenged this assumption by offering a more convenient, cost-effective, and reliable alternative. Despite initial resistance from the taxi industry, ride-hailing services eventually became mainstream and disrupted the traditional taxi industry.

In conclusion, remaining open-minded and willing to revise assumptions based on new evidence or perspectives is crucial for effective first principle thinking. By doing so, individuals can gain a more comprehensive understanding of a problem or situation and make informed decisions. Examples from medicine and business demonstrate the value of challenging assumptions and remaining open to new perspectives.

CHAPTER 15

Applying First Principle Thinking To Fields Beyond Science And Engineering: How First Principle Thinking Can Be Applied To Areas Like Philosophy, Business, And Politics.

1. Identify the fundamental principles underlying the field or subject matter you are exploring.

Identifying the fundamental principles underlying a field or subject matter is a key aspect of first principle thinking. By breaking down complex concepts into their foundational elements, it becomes easier to understand and analyze them.

For example, in the field of physics, one of the fundamental principles is the law of conservation of energy, which states that energy cannot be created or destroyed, only transferred or transformed from one form to another. This principle underlies many other laws and theories in physics, and understanding it is essential for making accurate predictions and explanations.

In the field of economics, the concept of supply and demand is a fundamental principle that underlies many economic theories and models. Understanding the relationship between supply and demand is crucial for making informed decisions about pricing, production, and resource allocation.

In order to identify these fundamental principles, it is important to do research and study the subject matter in depth. This may involve reading textbooks, scientific papers, and other sources of information, as well as consulting with experts in the field.

By identifying these fundamental principles, one can gain a deeper understanding of the subject matter and use first principle thinking to analyze and solve problems more effectively.

2. Analyze and evaluate the logic behind different theories and arguments in the field.

Analyzing and evaluating the logic behind different theories and arguments in a field is an important step in developing a deeper understanding of the subject matter. By examining the reasoning and evidence behind different arguments, one can better assess the strength of the argument and identify any flaws or weaknesses.

For example, in the field of climate change, there are various theories and arguments about the causes and impacts of global warming. Some argue that it is primarily caused by human activities such as burning fossil fuels, while others suggest that it is part of a natural cycle. By analyzing the evidence and reasoning behind these arguments, one can better understand the strength of each perspective.

A study by Cook et al. (2013) analyzed 11,944 scientific papers on climate change and found that 97.1% of the papers that took a position on the issue agreed that global warming is mainly caused by human activities. This highlights the strength of the argument that human activities are contributing to climate change.

Another example is in the field of economics, where there are various theories about how the economy works and what policies are most effective. By analyzing the reasoning and evidence behind these theories, one can better understand the strengths and weaknesses of each approach.

One study by Leamer (1983) analyzed the ability of different economic models to predict the future performance of the economy. The study found that no single model consistently outperformed the others, suggesting that there is no one-size-fits-all approach to economics.

Solutions:
To analyze and evaluate the logic behind different theories and arguments in a field, one can:

Read and study a variety of sources to gain a broad understanding of different perspectives.
Assess the evidence and reasoning behind different arguments.
Evaluate the assumptions underlying each argument and consider how they may affect the overall argument.
Consider the potential consequences of each perspective and evaluate their impact.
Seek out expert opinions and engage in discussion and debate to gain a deeper understanding of the subject matter.

3. *Question assumptions and biases that may be present in the field or subject matter.*

Questioning assumptions and biases is an essential part of critical thinking in any field. Here are some examples of how questioning assumptions and biases can be applied in different fields:

In medicine, assumptions and biases can have serious consequences for patient care. For example, a study found that physicians were more likely to prescribe pain medication to white patients than to black patients, even when controlling for other factors such as pain severity. By questioning assumptions and biases around race and pain, doctors can work to provide more equitable care to all patients.

In economics, assumptions about human behavior can impact policy decisions. For example, traditional economic models assume that people are rational and always act in their self-interest, but this assumption has been challenged by research showing that people often make irrational decisions and are motivated by factors beyond self-interest. By questioning these assumptions, economists can develop more accurate models and policies that better reflect human behavior.

In psychology, biases and assumptions can impact research findings and treatment approaches. For example, the field of psychology has historically been dominated by white, Western perspectives, which has led to biases in research and treatment approaches that may not be effective for people from different cultural backgrounds. By questioning these assumptions and biases, psychologists can work to develop more culturally sensitive and effective treatments.

Overall, questioning assumptions and biases is an important part of critical thinking in any field, as it can lead to more accurate theories, policies, and practices.

4. Apply first principles to generate new insights and perspectives on the field.

Applying first principles can lead to new insights and perspectives in a field, as it allows for a deeper understanding of the underlying principles and can reveal gaps or inconsistencies in current theories or practices. This approach has been used in a variety of fields to generate new ideas and solutions.

For example, in the field of renewable energy, applying first principles has led to the development of new materials and technologies that improve efficiency and reduce costs. One example is the use of perovskite solar cells, which are a relatively new technology that has the potential to be cheaper and more efficient than traditional silicon-based solar cells. Researchers applied first principles to identify the optimal composition and structure for perovskite materials, which led to the development of high-performance solar cells.

In the field of medicine, applying first principles has led to the development of new treatments and therapies. One example is the use of immunotherapy to treat cancer. Immunotherapy works by stimulating the immune system to attack cancer cells, but its effectiveness has been limited in some cases. Researchers applied first principles to understand the mechanisms behind the immune system's response to cancer, which led to the development of new therapies that improve its effectiveness.

In the field of economics, applying first principles has led to new insights on how the economy works and how to address economic challenges. One example is the development of behavioral economics, which applies first principles to understand how people make economic decisions. This approach has led to new insights on the role of emotions and social norms in economic decision-making, which has implications for policy and practice.

Overall, applying first principles can lead to new ideas and solutions in a variety of fields by providing a deeper understanding of the underlying principles and revealing gaps or inconsistencies in current theories or practices.

5. Use first principle thinking to identify potential problems or limitations in the current state of the field.

Using first principles thinking to identify potential problems or limitations in the current state of a field can be a powerful tool for innovation and improvement. By breaking down complex concepts into their fundamental components and questioning assumptions, one can often uncover underlying issues that may have been previously overlooked.

For example, in the field of healthcare, first principle thinking could be used to identify potential problems with the current model of care delivery. By breaking down the various components of healthcare, such as diagnosis, treatment, and follow-up care, and questioning the assumptions that underlie them, one might discover that certain aspects of the system are inefficient or ineffective. This could lead to new innovations, such as telemedicine or preventative care strategies, that could improve the overall quality of care.

Another example is in the field of renewable energy. By applying first principles thinking, one might identify potential limitations with existing technologies and approaches, such as the reliance on rare earth metals in solar panels or the intermittency of wind power. By breaking down these issues and questioning the underlying assumptions, researchers and engineers could develop new, more efficient and sustainable technologies that overcome these limitations.

Overall, the application of first principles thinking can help identify potential problems or limitations in any field, leading to new innovations and solutions.

6. Consider alternative approaches or frameworks based on first principles to address these problems or limitations.

When considering alternative approaches or frameworks based on first principles, it is important to evaluate them critically and objectively. One example of this is the field of renewable energy, where first principle thinking has led to the development of new technologies and approaches to generate and store clean energy.

For instance, one approach that has emerged is the use of nanotechnology in solar cells. Traditional solar cells rely on silicon, which can be expensive and not always efficient. However, researchers have developed nanotechnology-based solar cells that are more efficient and cost-effective. This approach is based on the first principle of using materials that can absorb light and convert it into energy.

Another example is the development of flow batteries for energy storage. Traditional batteries can be limited in their capacity and durability, but flow batteries use two liquid electrolytes separated by a membrane to store energy. This approach is based on the first principle of using a system that can store and release energy on demand.

Overall, applying first principle thinking to the field of renewable energy has led to innovative and sustainable solutions that have the potential to transform the industry.

7. Apply first principle thinking to identify opportunities for innovation or disruption in the field.

First principles thinking can also be applied to identify opportunities for innovation or disruption in a given field. By breaking down a problem or a product into its fundamental components and understanding the underlying principles, one can identify potential areas for improvement or entirely new approaches that may have been overlooked.

One notable example of this is Elon Musk's approach to space travel with SpaceX. Rather than simply trying to improve upon existing rocket designs, Musk and his team applied first principles thinking to question assumptions about the cost and feasibility of space travel. By breaking down the cost of rockets into their individual components and identifying ways to manufacture them more efficiently, SpaceX was able to drastically reduce the cost of space travel.

Similarly, first principles thinking can be applied to other industries and fields to identify opportunities for innovation and disruption. By questioning assumptions and understanding the fundamental principles underlying a particular field, one can identify potential areas for improvement or new approaches that may have been overlooked.

For example, the rise of electric vehicles (EVs) is a result of first principles thinking applied to the automotive industry. The fundamental principle behind gasoline-powered cars is the internal combustion engine, which has many limitations, including emissions and inefficiency. By breaking down the components of a car and understanding the principles behind electric power, innovators were able to create a completely new type of vehicle that has the potential to revolutionize transportation.

Overall, applying first principles thinking to a field can help identify opportunities for innovation and disruption, leading to new solutions that may not have been possible otherwise.

8. Use first principle thinking to generate new hypotheses or theories in the field.

First principle thinking can be a valuable tool for generating new hypotheses or theories in any field. By breaking down a problem or phenomenon into its fundamental components and building up from there, it is possible to arrive at novel insights and perspectives that may not have been immediately apparent.

For example, consider the field of psychology. One of the fundamental principles underlying this field is that human behavior is influenced by a combination of genetic, environmental, and cultural factors. Using first principle thinking, a psychologist might break down this principle into its component parts and explore each one in detail. They might ask questions like:

What specific genetic factors contribute to human behavior?
How do environmental factors such as upbringing and social context influence behavior?
How do cultural factors such as beliefs and values shape behavior?
By examining each of these components in detail, a psychologist might be able to generate new hypotheses or theories about human behavior that had not been considered before. For example, they might hypothesize that certain genetic variations are associated with higher levels of empathy, or that exposure to certain environmental toxins during childhood can lead to increased risk-taking behavior later in life.

These hypotheses can then be tested through empirical research, using methods such as surveys, experiments, and observational studies. If the results of these studies support the hypotheses, they can be further refined and developed into new theories or models of human behavior.

In this way, first principle thinking can be a powerful tool for advancing knowledge and understanding in any field, by encouraging researchers to think deeply and creatively about the underlying principles that govern their subject matter.

9. *Evaluate different ethical or moral frameworks in philosophy or politics based on first principles.*

Evaluating ethical or moral frameworks based on first principles involves analyzing the underlying values and principles that inform these frameworks. One approach to this is to consider the ethical principles of autonomy, beneficence, non-maleficence, and justice, which are widely used in healthcare ethics and have broader applications in other areas as well.

Autonomy refers to the principle that individuals have the right to make decisions about their own lives and bodies. Beneficence refers to the principle of doing good or promoting the well-being of others. Non-maleficence refers to the principle of avoiding harm or not causing harm to others. Justice refers to the principle of fairness and equality in the distribution of benefits and burdens.

For example, in evaluating different ethical frameworks related to healthcare, we can consider how each framework prioritizes these principles. A framework that prioritizes autonomy might emphasize patient-centered decision making and the right of individuals to make choices about their own healthcare. A framework that prioritizes beneficence might prioritize the provision of medical treatments that promote the health and well-being of patients. A framework that prioritizes non-maleficence might prioritize avoiding medical treatments that have harmful side effects or risks. A framework that prioritizes justice might prioritize equitable access to healthcare services for all individuals, regardless of their socioeconomic status or other factors.

In politics, the application of first principles can be used to evaluate different ethical or moral frameworks related to governance, social justice, and human rights. For example, a framework that prioritizes individual liberty and limited government might emphasize individual rights and freedoms, such as freedom of speech, religion, and association. A framework that prioritizes social justice might emphasize the importance of reducing inequality and promoting equal opportunities for all members of society. A framework that prioritizes human rights might emphasize the protection of basic human rights, such as the right to life, liberty, and security of person.

In all cases, applying first principle thinking can help to identify the underlying values and principles that inform different ethical or moral frameworks, and to evaluate them based on their logical consistency and coherence. It can also help to identify potential limitations or shortcomings in these frameworks, and to generate new ideas and approaches based on alternative principles and values.

10. Use first principle thinking to identify opportunities for growth and improvement in business strategy or operations.

First principle thinking can be an effective tool for identifying opportunities for growth and improvement in business strategy or operations. By breaking down complex problems into their fundamental components, it becomes possible to identify new approaches and solutions that might not have been immediately apparent.

For example, consider a company that is struggling to increase its profit margins. Using first principle thinking, the company might start by examining the basic components that contribute to its costs and revenues. This could include identifying inefficiencies in the supply chain, exploring new pricing models, or identifying new market opportunities that the company has not yet considered.

One example of a company that has successfully used first principle thinking to drive growth and innovation is SpaceX, the rocket company founded by entrepreneur Elon Musk. By breaking down the fundamental principles of rocket engineering and space travel, SpaceX was able to identify new approaches and technologies that have disrupted the traditional aerospace industry.

For instance, SpaceX has focused on developing reusable rockets that can be landed and used again, dramatically reducing the cost of space travel. This approach was initially met with skepticism from industry experts who believed that it would be impossible to make rockets reusable, but SpaceX was able to overcome these challenges by applying first principle thinking to the problem.

Overall, first principle thinking can be a powerful tool for identifying opportunities for growth and improvement in business strategy or operations. By breaking down complex problems into their fundamental components, it becomes possible to identify new approaches and solutions that might not have been immediately apparent using conventional thinking.

CONCLUSION

Generate a comprehensive conclusion for the above book, "Think Outside the Books: A Guide to First Principle Thinking"

In conclusion, "Think Outside the Books: A Guide to First Principle Thinking" provides readers with a comprehensive understanding of the importance of first principle thinking in various aspects of life, including philosophy, science, business, and everyday decision-making. The book encourages readers to challenge assumptions, question conventional wisdom, and seek out diverse perspectives to develop innovative solutions and insights.

Through numerous examples, case studies, and exercises, readers can apply the principles of first principle thinking to their lives and work, and generate new ideas and perspectives. By adopting a systematic, logical, and creative approach to problem-solving, readers can navigate complex challenges and make informed decisions based on fact and sound reasoning.

This book aims to inspire readers to think beyond the surface level and approach problems with a fresh perspective. By cultivating critical thinking skills, practicing creative brainstorming techniques, and applying first principle thinking to everyday challenges, readers can unlock their full potential and achieve greater success in their personal and professional lives.

In a world that is constantly changing, it is crucial to have the tools to adapt and thrive. "Think Outside the Books: A Guide to First Principle Thinking" equips readers with the mindset and skills to navigate uncertainty and complexity with confidence, creativity, and curiosity.